Youth Civic Engagement and Local Peacebuilding in the Middle East and North Africa

This book investigates the ways in which young people engage with and contribute to civil society, community development, and local peacebuilding in the Middle East and North Africa (MENA).

Youth engagement and contribution to civil society and local peacebuilding can play a crucial role in development; however, there is often a lack of effective engagement, policies, and opportunities for young people in policy and practice. This book analyses their experiences of civic engagement and community participation and the challenges they face, across diverse areas including youth empowerment, freedom of expression, mobilization, ideologies, conflict resolution, and peacebuilding. Drawing on cases from Yemen, Syria, Iran, Morocco, and the Palestinian Territories, this book offers new insights on how youth not only are shaped by, but also react to policies, conflict, constraints, and challenges.

The insights drawn from this interdisciplinary collection will be of interest to researchers of civil society, youth, peacebuilding, and development, as well as to policymakers, donors, and NGO staff.

Ibrahim Natil is a Research Fellow at Institute of International Conflict Resolution and Reconstruction (IICRR) and teaches at Dublin City University, Ireland. He is the Co-convenor of NGOs in Development Study Group, DSA-UK, and winner of the Robert Chamber Best Overall Paper, selected by DSA Ireland (2017). He is the founder of the Society Voice Foundation for Community Work.

T0347546

Routledge Explorations in Development Studies

This Development Studies series features innovative and original research at the regional and global scale. It promotes interdisciplinary scholarly works drawing on a wide spectrum of subject areas, in particular politics, health, economics, rural and urban studies, sociology, environment, anthropology, and conflict studies.

Topics of particular interest are globalization; emerging powers; children and youth; cities; education; media and communication; technology development; and climate change.

In terms of theory and method, rather than basing itself on any orthodoxy, the series draws broadly on the tool kit of the social sciences in general, emphasizing comparison, the analysis of the structure and processes, and the application of qualitative and quantitative methods.

Philanthropic Foundations in International Development
Rockefeller, Ford and Gates
Patrick Kilby

Foreign Aid and Development in South Korea and Africa
A Comparative Analysis of Economic Growth
Kelechi A. Kalu and Jiyoung Kim

Women and the UN
A New History of Women's International Human Rights
Edited by Rebecca Adami and Dan Plesch

Youth Civic Engagement and Local Peacebuilding in the Middle East and North Africa
Prospects and Challenges for Community Development
Edited by Ibrahim Natil

For more information about this series, please visit: www.routledge.com/ Routledge-Explorations-in-Development-Studies/book-series/REDS

Youth Civic Engagement and Local Peacebuilding in the Middle East and North Africa

Prospects and Challenges for Community Development

Edited by Ibrahim Natil

Routledge
Taylor & Francis Group

LONDON AND NEW YORK

First published 2021
by Routledge
2 Park Square, Milton Park, Abingdon, Oxon OX14 4RN

and by Routledge
605 Third Avenue, New York, NY 10158

Routledge is an imprint of the Taylor & Francis Group, an Informa business

British Library Cataloguing-in-Publication Data
A catalogue record for this book is available from the British Library

Library of Congress Cataloging-in-Publication Data
Names: Natil, Ibrahim, editor.
Title: Youth civic engagement and local peacebuilding in the Middle East and North Africa: prospects and challenges for community development/ Ibrahim Natil.
Description: New York: Routledge, 2021. |
Series: Routledge explorations in development studies |
Includes bibliographical references and index.
Identifiers: LCCN 2021006647 (print) | LCCN 2021006648 (ebook)
Subjects: LCSH: Youth–Political activity–Africa, North. |
Youth–Political activity–Middle East. | Social action–Africa, North. |
Social action–Middle East. | Political participation–Africa, North. |
Political participation–Middle East. | Community development–Africa,
North. | Community development–Middle East.
Classification: LCC HQ799.A35 Y68 2021 (print) | LCC HQ799.A35
(ebook) | DDC 320.0835/0956–dc23
LC record available at https://lccn.loc.gov/2021006647
LC ebook record available at https://lccn.loc.gov/2021006648

ISBN: 978-1-032-02521-6 (hbk)
ISBN: 978-1-032-02526-1 (pbk)
ISBN: 978-1-003-18374-7 (ebk)

Typeset in Times New Roman
by Deanta Global Publishing Services, Chennai, India

Contents

Contributors

Belal Abdo is a former diplomat at Yemen's Mission to the United Nations in New York, in charge of the political and economic portfolios. He holds an MA in Conflict and Humanitarian Studies. His research interests include governance, statebuilding, and state formation; civil wars; rebel groups and militias; security studies; conflict resolution; and post-conflict reconstruction in the Middle East region.

Abdulrahman Abohajeb is a researcher currently working with Search for Common Ground (Search) in Yemen. He holds an MA in Conflict Management and Humanitarian Action. He has worked in different capacities with several organizations including MSF and Plan International.

Wadee Alarabeed is a human rights activist, skilled in analysis, critical thinking, writing reports, and legal writing. He has a BA in law and worked as a lawyer at the Palestinian Centre for Human Rights (PCHR). He holds an MA in Conflict Management and Humanitarian Action from the Doha Institute for Graduate Studies.

Ola Alkahlout is a PhD candidate at Coventry University. Her research examines the theological and sociological influences of the everyday lived experience of *Zakāt* practice in contemporary Qatar (2017–2020). She holds an MS in Islamic Banking, Finance, and Management from the University of Gloucestershire.

Hamza Bailla is a freelance journalist and researcher interested in digital media, politics, and interfaith dialogue. He graduated from the university of Moulay Ismail with a Master's degree in communication in contexts: culture and dialogue.

Nader Ganji is a university lecturer in Iran. He holds a PhD in Public Policy from the University of Tehran. He published a number of journal articles on pressure groups, organized religion and Iran's government policies. He has written a book on Public Policy and Pressure Groups as well as a forthcoming book chapter on the Political Structure of Iran.

Alaa Hadid completed his MA in Conflict Management and Humanitarian Action at the Doha Institute for Graduate Studies. She worked as a consultant for the Danish Refugee Council (DRC) in the South Caucasus, Abkhazia, Georgia. She worked in the Ministry of Foreign Affairs of Abkhazia, Georgia in the external relations department and with the International Crisis Group in Europe and Central Asia department focussing on the South Caucasus region.

Yousra Hasona is a Palestinian lawyer and researcher. She holds an MA in criminal law and is interested in researching issues relating to child soldiers and restorative justice, especially in the Arab Spring countries.

Ala Mohsen is a Political Science PhD student. Ala's areas of interest include Middle East politics (with extensive focus on Yemen and the Gulf states), IR theory, foreign policy, conflict studies, and public policy. Substantially, Ala studies civil wars, rebel movements, and Islamist groups.

Mohsen Moheimany holds a PhD in Political Science and International Relations from Dublin City University (2019). He is a political journalist and researcher and has published a number of articles and book chapters on developments of the Islamic Republic of Iran.

Ibrahim Natil is a research fellow at the Institute of International Conflict Resolution and Reconstruction (IICRR) and teaches politics at CTYI, Dublin City University (DCU). He is the Co-convenor of NGOs in Development Study Group, DSA-UK, and winner of the Robert Chamber Best Overall Paper, selected by DSA Ireland (2017). He is the author of *Conflict, Civil Society, and Women's Empowerment* (2021) and *Hamas Transformation Opportunities and Challenges* (2015). He is the leading editor of books: *Barriers to Effective Civil Society Organisations: Political, Social and Funding Shifts* (Routledge, 2020) and the *Power of Civil Society in the Middle East and North Africa: Peacebuilding, Change and Development* (Routledge, 2019). He writes for *Independent Australia* and has published several articles and book chapters. He also has worked for many international INGOs and CSOs, managed more than 60 civil society projects since 1997.

Elham Raweh is a project manager at Saferworld – a leading NGO working in preventing violent conflict. She worked with several NGOs as a consultant, manager, coordinator, trainer, and facilitator. She holds an MA in Conflict Management and Humanitarian Assistance. She is an activist, researcher, and consultant in Yemeni affairs.

Morvarid Salehi practiced law for several years and is an experienced Attorney at Law based in Iran. Being a member of the Iranian Bar Association, she has been working as a lawyer specializing in various legal fields. She holds an LLB and is a graduate of the University of Tehran. Her main area of interest includes policymaking and the political system in contemporary Iran.

Mohammed Yachoulti is an associate professor at the School of Arts and Human Sciences, Moulay Ismail University of Meknes – Morocco. His recent publications include "Shifting Landscape in Morocco: The Case of Civil Society Activism in Post 2011 Uprisings," "Migration Reform in Morocco: Political and social realities behind the 2013 law," "Moroccan women's resistance to *Al-hogra* in the aftermaths of Arab Spring," "Syrian refugees in Morocco: Realities and prospects," and "Women of February 20th movement in Morocco."

Introduction

Ibrahim Natil

The World Youth Report (2016) on youth civic engagement by the Department of Economic and Social Affairs of the United Nations Secretariat uses the term "youth" to refer to all those aged between 15 and 24. The term "young people" is used interchangeably with the word "youth." This book, however, explores the roles, contributions, and challenges of young people aged 18–30 years old on civic engagement, community development, and local peacebuilding. Young people are considered a major segment of society who have a considerable impact and influence on their societies in times of both peace and conflict. Youths' engagement with and contribution to development and local peacebuilding play a crucial role in international development; however, they have a limited impact on policy and practice and, ultimately, the lives of poor youths owing to a lack of effective engagement, policies, and opportunities, as the World Youth Report (2016) discusses. Berents and McEvoy-Levy (2015) discuss everyday youth peacebuilding, their age, and structures that facilitate everyday peacebuilding practices. They also consider the activities, civil society organizations (CSOs) and initiatives led by young people by focussing on the youths' positive role in reference to peace and security agendas and UN Security Council Resolution 2250 (2015). Young people's engagement in CSOs, outlining the problems and challenges that exist, is part of the solution concerning increasing the influence and impact of their work.

The book focuses on three themes: civic engagement, local peacebuilding, and development. By examining specific youth case studies in Yemen, Syria, Iran, the Palestinian Territories, and Morocco, it aims at improving our understanding of how these issues/themes are influencing the way the youth and their CSOs contribute, deliver, intervene, and position themselves in various societies. Particular emphasis is placed upon the different challenges faced by youths from different locations that are linked not only to conflict constraints but also to technical issues and policies that are crucial markers of engagement and change. Remarkably, although considerable research has highlighted the weaknesses and limitations of youth influence and power, rather less attention has been paid to the policies and conflicts that result in the exceptional circumstances and dynamics characterizing some societies in which youths and their CSOs find themselves. Therefore, the book offers new insights on how youths in these countries are not only shaped by but also react to policies, conflicts, constraints, and challenges.

This book primarily contains research that provides up-to-date analysis on youths' civic engagement and community participation, social and political challenges, empowerment, and peacebuilding. However, it also pays particular attention to young women to highlight their impact on young people's engagement in peacebuilding and development. Young groups of women aged 18–30 years old also play an active role in young people's engagement (Chapter 7 highlights this issue). Youth integration and community practice through social justice, service-learning, and civic engagement is a conceptual and philosophical foundation, as discussed by Melvin Deldado (2016). Young people, however, may view their representation process as an outcome of civic empowerment according to the cultural context of their society. This empowerment can be understood through the lenses of security, transformative change, and participation (Porter, 2013). This can be reflected by a "participatory democracy" process, as Hilmer (2010) and Aragones and Sánchez-Pagés (2009) discuss. A civic "participatory democracy" process is also associated with the practice of a top-down mechanism conducted to include young people's engagement and contribution to the public sector, as Bherer, Dufour, and Montambeault (2016) argue. Developing civic engagement in urban public art programmes is a significant process for youth empowerment (DeShazo and Smith, 2017).

The concept of "participatory democracy" is discussed to explore where active young people have the power to decide on changes for their future. The book here considers an examination of the power of young people's leadership, the impact of their network and coordination, and their undertaking of effective actions and campaigns in order to make change a reality in terms of peace, security, and development (Pruitt and Lee-Koo, 2020). This will assist the reader to understand young people's capacities, contributions, challenges, and role in civic engagement and local peacebuilding (Ozerdem and Podder, 2015; Honwana, 2013). In other words, the book discusses the significance of the relationship between local peacebuilding and community development and the impact of youth civic engagement and local peacebuilding on community development. It also critically examines the post-conflict approach by exploring the challenges facing young people in reference to civic engagement and local peacebuilding (McEvoy-Levy 2006; Ozerdem and Podder, 2015).

The chapters explore the lessons gained from youth civic engagement despite repressive regimes, violence, social conservatism, lack of opportunities, and the impact of various political systems (United Nations, 2016; CIVICUS, 2020). They also examine these experiences and case studies of youth engagement in the civil society activities of local peacebuilding and community development. The chapters analyse the extent to which the youth are equipped by social media and various technology platforms to facilitate the organization of protests as well as the framing of political and social demands discussed by the World Youth Report (2016). They also examine the impact of CSOs on youth politics, power, and social and political life. The active engagement and contributions of young people to community peacebuilding, development, human rights, politics, and change processes at different levels are varied and contextual (Natil, 2019, 2020). Some of the obstacles that face youths' contributions that hinder their ability to perform their engagement are the policy processes that exist in some developing countries. These processes often undermine young people's engagement and block their CSOs' operations and deliveries. In many contexts, however, it is largely about the ways youth engagement in civil society works. In short, this book raises and addresses the following questions: How do the region's cultures and backgrounds perceive the youth and their engagement in local politics? To what extent has youth civic engagement contributed to local peacebuilding and development processes?

This book also aims to demonstrate how CSOs led by youths or serving youths are currently engaging in various contexts, which will provide important observations for different target groups, including scientists, researchers, national-level policymakers, donors, NGO staff, and the beneficiaries themselves. Each of these groups has different communication needs. This book will be highly influential as it contains in-depth understandings and evidence of particular youths' engagement in development and community peacebuilding actions. Its presentation of up-to-date empirical research will help readers to understand the significance of youths' engagement with and contribution to CSOs' actions in the fields of development, peacebuilding, and civic engagement. It also aims to highlight the significant work performed by youths and their CSOs as well as their credibility across global contexts, proving they have earned their right to sit at the policymaking table. It brings together case studies from various countries, sharing diverse challenges experienced by youths and/or their CSOs in areas such as political and social contexts, leadership, networking, expertise, and sustainability. It also explores in detail the factors and challenges of political, social, and funding shifts which influence the youth and civil society sectors.

It provides insight into the engagement of factors, circumstances, and historical changes that influence the development and activities of civil society, as well as the organizational, financial, and political challenges facing the sector today. Specifically, the book provides up-to-date analysis on civic engagement, local peacebuilding, and community participation challenges and lessons in Yemen, Syria, Iran, the Palestinian Territories, and Morocco. It is innovative and different as it mainly stems from the experiences and fieldwork of young contributors from these regions, enriching the debate on various developments with new insights and fresh perspectives, particularly from the Global South. It also provides the reader with empirically based, up to date but still scientifically grounded analyses of civil society developments in countries of MENA that will be appealing not only to an academic audience but also to international agencies, policymakers, and practitioners active in the region.

The nine chapters are structured around the theme of youth development action and practice, and they are further subdivided into the themes of civic engagement, active participation, and local peacebuilding to make the edited volume more coherent. An introductory chapter and conclusion are also included, and these provide a sound theoretical and structural framework for the reader's benefit into which each individual case study chapter is placed. The introduction and conclusion also place the scope of the book into the wider academic discussion about the topic, so there are clear references to related materials and themes within which this book is situated. The chapters are empirical, but each one also discusses the theories and methodologies relevant to its country case study. Therefore, a balance between theoretical/methodological and empirical discussions is ensured. Natil's chapter (Chapter 1) covers the background, framework, scope, and questions of the study and its methods. It introduces explorations of young people's engagement and practices as well as shedding light on their challenges in contemporary societies. It focuses on three themes/constraints – civic engagement, local peacebuilding, and community development – and, by examining specific case studies, aims at improving our understanding of the challenges facing young people and their CSOs in various societies. In short, this chapter raises and addresses the following questions: To what extent have young people actually succeeded in achieving their objectives despite the technical and policy challenges? What is the role of civil society in overcoming the challenges facing youth civic engagement, community development, and local peacebuilding? How have local and grassroots youth organizations overcome challenges in their societies?

Chapter 1 introduces the concepts of youth civic engagement and local peacebuilding and prospects and challenges for community development. This chapter by Natil introduces the theoretical framework, exploring technical constraints and policies and their impact on youth civic engagement, active participation, and local peacebuilding and how these can be understood. The three sections – civic engagement, community development, and local peacebuilding – speak clearly about these definitions and concepts in reference to the existing literature. The chapter brings some figures from relevant UN agencies, reputable research groups, and international organizations about the status of youths in the MENA region. Natil also discusses the existing literature to explore and compare the definitions of civic engagement and local peacebuilding.

Young people's representation and engagement in grassroots activities can help to promote their contribution to decision-making processes and give them a platform to decide on changes to their societies despite conflicts, a lack of policies, restrictive political environments, and the complexity of their sociocultural and economic contexts (United Nations, 2016; CIVICUS, 2020; Natil, 2019, 2020). The impact of the political environment and conflict on youth engagement and their contribution to local peacebuilding in the Gaza Strip is introduced by Ola Alkahlout in Chapter 2. Alkahlout's chapter explores how the youth could engage in local peacebuilding initiatives with CSOs' support and the impact of young people's civic engagement and local peacebuilding on these initiatives and challenges to community development. Young people are an important part of society, having a considerable impact and influence in times of both peace and conflict, yet they are not included in decision-making processes, community development, or peacebuilding programmes. Could CSOs help the youth as participants in the Gaza Strip to improve their social situation according to the local environment? There are a number of grassroots initiatives and CSOs led by young people, and Alkahlout discusses some of these initiatives.

Conflict influences young people's engagement; however, Covid-19 and the political context have already affected youth social movements in Iran, as Mohsen Moheimany, Nader Ganji, and Morvarid Salehi discuss in Chapter 3. The contributors take the Covid-19 outbreak in Iran as a case study of how the crisis turned into an opportunity for the authoritarian leaders to employ the force of the youth in semi-military capacities, namely the Basij. They also discuss the impact of young people's civic engagement on local politics and community development based on their research and engagement there. Following a review of the literature on patron-client networks in undemocratic regimes, the chapter looks at several waves of mobilization of loyal youth movements in the contemporary history of Iran. Afterwards, it explains how the crisis has led to further authoritarianism through militarization by means of the engagement of social networks.

Social networks, however, have become sites of an unprecedented diffusion of fake news and misinformation, as Mohammed Yachoulti and Hamza Baila discuss in Chapter 4 with regard to youths' virtual activism in Morocco. This fact not only affects people as individuals but also undermines social order and cohesion in general. To fight back, a number of individuals have emerged both as citizen journalists and activists to engage in fact-checking processes not only to verify claims and information but also to promote a healthier public debate in the contemporary media environment and set the stage for movements to grow. This study considers fact-checking as an emerging journalistic brand and activism that has the potential to correct inconveniences in the public sphere and establish a common ethical consensus. The significance of this chapter resides in the fact that it tracks this issue in the Moroccan media landscape and investigates its importance in creating communities of interest. Civil society activists, for example, use social media networks to overcome the shortcomings of representative democracy that has failed to achieve their aspiration of ending violence and internal divisions (Natil, 2017).

These challenges impose major barriers to effective youth civic engagement and community development in Syria, where conflict has weakened the country and destroyed society, as Alaa Hadid discusses in Chapter 5. These actions have not always been welcomed as the political atmosphere in the country is highly polarized. Many challenges face those young people who are involved in civic engagement, change, and community development in Syria. The conflict also influences the most vulnerable groups, as some children are being used by the warlords. Children's integration and rehabilitation in a post-conflict process remain significant for society's stability and future development prospects. In Chapter 6, Yousra Hasona identifies child soldiers of the 15–17 age group who are considered "youths" in some Arab cultures and contexts and discusses this group in the post-conflict phase. This age group, who will be "youths" in a couple of years, is considered a serious challenge for peacebuilding and community development processes. This chapter aims at looking more deeply into how restorative justice can be used as a new approach to deal with child soldiers. Restorative justice is a method used within criminal matters to achieve justice in a different way to the usual application of criminal justice. In different countries like Iraq and Libya, child soldiers are treated like criminals, and the authorities keep them in detention without trial. This chapter also discusses the impact of these children on the local peacebuilding and development process.

The impact of conflict also hinders young women's activism and involvement in a changing environment, as Belal Abdo, Abdulrahman Abohajeb, and Ala Mohsen discuss in Chapter 7 with regard to the Yemeni conflict. This chapter provides a hint about the impact of the 2011 uprisings in the Arab world that have unleashed significant social and political changes in the region. They endeavour to address the transformation of women's roles from non-violent participation to direct armed engagement by shedding light on the repercussions of the militarization of women in Yemeni society. Elham Raweh also discusses Yemeni youths' transition from uprising to fragile political engagement in Chapter 8. This chapter is an attempt to enrich the field of peacebuilding literature with a critical examination of the implementation of UNSCR 2250 and its complementary resolutions 2419 (2018) and 2535 (2020) in the Yemeni context, analysing its successes and failures in bringing Yemeni youth to the peace process.

Young people who live in the Gaza Strip also suffer from different circumstances owing to the political conflict between the Palestinians and Israel. Wadee Alarabeed examines youth participation in post-conflict reconstruction efforts in the Gaza Strip in Chapter 9. Alarabeed explains the relationship between youth participation and post-war reconstruction initiatives, describing how the Gazan youth were excluded from the reconstruction process that has taken place in the Gaza Strip since the 2014 war. The participation of the local community, including its youth, is set at the heart of reconstruction initiatives, and so youth participation should have been a main pillar in the post-war reconstruction efforts.

By assessing the different contexts and engaging policymakers with rigorous empirical research in a systematic way, youth engagement can work to overcome both the internal and external challenges they face. Natil's concluding chapter assesses the research's implications and future directions. This book provides insights and hopes to stimulate others to conduct further investigations into this growing area of research. It concludes with some implications and offers some direction for future research in the fields of young people's engagement, contribution, and deliveries in non-Western contexts. It also introduces the lessons learnt from young people's engagement and contribution in responding to technical constraints and improper policies, despite the existence of social conservatism, conflict, violence and the absence of democracy and exclusive political systems in a number of countries. Through extensive desk reviews and in-depth interviews with different stakeholders, young scholars from MENA countries provide up-to-date analyses on youth civic engagement, community participation, and local peacebuilding challenges and lessons learnt therefrom.

References

Aragones, E. and Sánchez-Pagés, S. (2009). A theory of participatory democracy based on the real case of Porto Alegre, *European Economic Review*, 53:1, 56–72.

Berents, B. and McEvoy-Levy, S. (2015). Theorising youth and everyday peace(building), *Peacebuilding*, 3:2, 115–125, DOI: 10.1080/21647259.2015.1052627.

Bherer, L., Dufour, P., and Montambeault, F. (2016). The participatory democracy turn: an introduction. *Journal of Civil Society*, 12:3, 225–230, DOI:10.1080/17448689.2016.1216383.

CIVICUS (2020). State of Civil Society Report 2020. Accessed on January 14, 2021 https://www.civicus.org/documents/reports-and-publications/SOCS/2020/SOCS2020_Executive_Summary_en.pdf.

Deldado, M. (2016). *Community Practice and Urban Youth: Social Justice Service-Learning and Civic*. Routledge.

DeShazo, J. and Smith, Z. (2017). *Developing Civic Engagement in Urban Public Art Programs*. Rowman & Littlefield Publishers.

Hilmer, J. (2010). The state of participatory democratic theory, *New Political Science*, 32:1, 43–63, DOI: 10.1080/07393140903492118.

Honwana, A. (2013) *Youth and Revolution in Tunisia*. Zed Books.

McEvoy-Levy, S. (2006). *Troublemakers or Peacemakers: Youth and Post-Accord Peacebuilding*. University of Notre Dame Press.

Natil, I. (2017). Youth movement and Arab spring. pp. 33–42. In Arbatli, E. and Rosenberg, D. (Eds), *Non-Western Social Movements and Participatory Democracy in the Age of Transnationalism*. Springer.

Natil, I. (2019). The power of civil society: young leaders' engagement in non-violent actions in Palestine. pp. 24–36. In Natil, I., Pieroban, C., and Tauber, L. (Eds), *The Power of Civil Society in the Middle East and North Africa: Peacebuilding, Change and Development*. New York, NY: Routledge.

Natil, I. (2020). Introducing barriers to effective civil society organisations. pp. 9–17. In Natil, I., Malila, V., and Sai, Y. (Eds), *Barriers to Effective Civil Society Organisations: Political, Social and Financial Shifts*. New York, NY: Routledge.

Ozerdem, A. and Podder S. (2015). *Youth in Conflict and Peacebuilding*. Palgrave

Porter, E. (2013). Rethinking women's empowerment, *Journal of Peacebuilding & Development*, 8:1, 1–14, DOI: 10.1080/15423166.2013.785657.

Pruitt, L. and Lee-Koo, K. (2020). *Young Women and Leadership*. Routledge.

United Nations (2016). *The World Youth Report. Youth Civic Engagement*. Department of Economic and Social Affairs of the United Nations Secretariat. Accessed on January 13, 2021 https://www.un.org/development/desa/youth/wp-content/uploads/sites/21/2018/12/un_world_youth_report_youth_civic_engagement.pdf.

1 Introducing challenges to youth civic engagement and local peacebuilding

Ibrahim Natil

Introduction

This chapter discusses the challenges of young people's engagement, which is defined as their power to cope with and contribute to their societies. It also discusses the existing literature to explore and compare the definitions of civic engagement, community development, and local peacebuilding. Civil society organizations (CSOs), representation, and engagement in grassroots activities can help promote young people's contribution to decision-making processes and give them a platform to decide on changes to their society despite conflicts, a lack of policies, restrictive political environments, and the complexity of the sociocultural and economic contexts. This will assist the reader to understand young people's capacities, contributions, challenges, and role in civic engagement and local peacebuilding (Ozerdem and Podder, 2015; Honwana, 2013).

Civic Engagement

UNICEF defines civic engagement as "individual or collective actions in which people participate to improve the well-being of communities or society in general" (Cho et al. 2020, p. 6). Young people, however, may view their representation as an outcome of empowerment according to the cultural context of their society. Youth organizations' representation and engagement in grassroots activities can help promote young people's contribution to decision-making processes and give them a platform to decide on changes to their society. This empowerment can be viewed through the lenses of security, transformative change, and participation (Porter, 2013). This can be understood as a form of "participatory democracy," as defined by Hilmer (2010) and Aragones and Sánchez-Pagés (2009). Is youth CSOs' activism, however, considered a form of grassroots engagement and a process of "participatory democracy?" Activism promotes civic participation, freedom of expression, and strengthening the basis for civil society dialogue and democratic discourse, with particular emphasis on the role of activists in a media environment (Spurk, 2010, pp. 3–29).

This chapter looks at the activities, efforts, and endeavours made by local CSOs to achieve the various objectives of young people's engagement by organizing capacity-building training activities, community monitoring and advocacy, research and field studies, awareness, and media releases. Michels and de Graaf (2010) discuss citizens' civil involvement, which has a number of positive effects such as social inclusion, civic skills and virtues, deliberation, and legitimacy. Youth CSOs endeavour to make training and campaigning activities as creative as possible to enhance activists' engagement in community participation actions. Is youths' active participation in local organizations, student unions, social movements, CSOs, and NGOs a form of "participatory democracy" in responding to the lack of a democratic process in a conflict zone or under a repressive regime? Polletta (2016) discusses the participatory enthusiasm of and impetus for engagement, where youths can practise their skills and knowledge freely to change their lives. Moreover, engagement is a significant tool for strengthening the public sphere, which is "made up of private people gathered together as a public and articulating the needs of society with the state," as discussed by Habermas (1991, p. 176; 1996).

This is a framework that has at its core the principles of participatory democracy, wherein some CSOs ensure that the implementation of activities remains inclusive and as broad-based as possible (Spurk, 2010, pp. 3–26). This framework presents the lived experiences of grassroots activists/peacebuilders and how they contribute to promoting and increasing young people's participatory contributions to decision-making processes and increasing their power to decide on changes to their own future. This empowerment can be understood through the lenses of security, transformative change, and participation (Porter, 2013), while Pruitt and Lee-Koo (2020) also discuss young women's leadership in times of peace and security. How can this be achieved via the contribution of active young people and their local CSOs, community groups, and political engagement? Some youth local organizations or CSOs often attempt to explore new spaces for young activists' social and political engagement by managing community development and post-conflict reconstruction, as well as by improving young people's engagement in policymaking processes, as discussed in Chapters 2 and 9. The young people's participatory process is also associated with the practice of a top-down mechanism conducted to include citizens' engagement and contribution to the public sector, as Bherer et al. (2016) argue. The CEO of the Crown Prince Foundation, Dr Tamam Mango, said:

> Engagement through volunteering allows individuals to grow through different experiences and gain skills that may help them in their future

endeavors. Through helping their community, young people can gain confidence in their leadership skills and become motivated to succeed (UNICEF, 2020).

Mullard and Aarvik (2020), however, argue that civil society has explored new civic spaces through increasing engagement on social media networks during the coronavirus pandemic. COVID-19's spread enforced activists to halt their civil protest actions and turn to social media engagement. Freedom of expression is a viable option for articulating citizens' discontent, as Youngs and Panchulidze (2020, pp. 11–20) discuss. Youngs and Panchulidze (2020, p. 4) add, however, that weak democracies and autocracies have used restrictive measures concerning COVID-19 to curb democratic activities and silence critical voices. In Chapter 3, Moheimany, Ganji, and Salehi discuss COVID-19, the youth, and engineered social movements in Iran, considering the COVID-19 outbreak in Iran as a case study of how the crisis turned into an opportunity for the authoritarian leaders to employ the force of the youth in semi-military capacities, namely the Basij, and how the crisis led to further authoritarianism through militarization by means of the engagement of the youth. The transparency of accessing information and data, which is essential to tracking and containing the spread of COVID-19, is limited in conflict zones (Peters and Taraboulsi-McCarthy, 2020). Some regimes have been found to control youth engagement and their CSOs' civic space by dominating financial channels (CIVICUS, 2020; Natil, 2020a; Weeden, 2015).

This book also considers examinations of the power of young people's leadership and their impact on networks, as well as their coordination and undertaking of effective actions and campaigns, in order to make change a reality in terms of peace, security, and development (Pruitt and Lee-Koo, 2020). Young people's engagement is based on their existing local networks (both virtual and non-virtual platforms) and building new coalitions. Youth CSOs may consider partnerships to promote the local ownership of activities on the ground and to introduce change (Natil, 2016, 2019, 2020a). The guiding principles of the intervention of CSOs working at the grassroots level rely on networking, cooperation, and coordination as key methods of programme implementation (Paffenholz, 2010).

The use of networks is to ensure the implementation of effective methodologies to interact with young participants and to encourage them to share their thoughts and engage in roleplay and simulations based on real-life experiences (Natil, 2016, 2019, 2020a). Michels and de Graaf (2010) discuss the development of civic skills, the increase of public engagement, and the opportunity to meet the demands of neighbourhoods and resolve their problems. This includes young people's engagement in voluntary work by using digital platforms and their personal networks to mobilize available financial and in-kind resources to render services to their communities in the current circumstances. Alkatary (2014) comments that local media outlets are reflections of any given community and that all community issues should top the agendas of those outlets. Local media networks have noticeably been attracted by the new approaches of young community peacemakers and their achievements in the field of local peacemaking.

The UN's World Youth Report (2016) discusses the increasing usage of new information and communication technologies and social media platforms by today's youth that have already effectively reshaped their activism both within and across borders. Cho et al. (2020) also discuss digital civic engagement by young people; however, the challenge of COVID-19 is considered a barrier to effective youth community engagement. Moreover, young people have been very resilient to the current circumstances of the pandemic. UNICEF's Jordan representative, Tanya Chapuisat, said:

> This has been an exceptionally difficult year, especially for young people whose entire lives, from study to work to socializing, have been upended. I am inspired by the resilience and the leadership shown by the youth volunteers who refused to let this pandemic break their spirit, instead they volunteered online to share lifesaving information, packed food parcels and took care of the most vulnerable in their community.
>
> (UNICEF, 2020).

Hundreds of young activists innovated a new approach by using their cars to protest against the Lebanese government's policy in the pandemic as online engagement cannot be a substitute for street protests in Lebanon (Youngs and Panchulidze, 2020, pp. 11–20). However, challenges to youth civic engagement, community development, and peacebuilding in Syria are characterised by a range of social, economic and political differences, as shown by Alaa Hadid in Chapter 5. Social networks have become the sites of an unprecedented diffusion of fake news and misinformation, as Yachoulti and Baila discuss in Chapter 4. Michels and de Graaf (2010) argue that "citizen participation serves an instrumental rather than an expressive purpose; in practice, participation is not regarded as a value in itself." This introduces the importance of activism as a realm of freedom from the state, and the state itself guarantees the public sphere, as Habermas argues (1991, 1996). These activities would broaden the base of support for civic engagement through the promotion of communication and understanding of the key elements of empowerment. Local CSOs have implemented activities to target and educate a large number of young people on the values of community peacebuilding.

Local peacebuilding

The role of youths' civic and political engagement and contribution to processes of change has been a significant issue to consider since the Arab Spring and the Tunisia Uprising in particular, as Honwana (2013) argues. However, young people's voices and experiences are still far from finding their full integration or understanding, as discussed by Berents and McEvoy-Levy (2015). This also includes the examination of youths in the post-conflict approach by exploring the challenges facing young people in reference to local peacebuilding (Ozerdem and Podder, 2015). Porter (2007) argues that complex issues of memory, truth, silence, and redress should be further explored while new ideas on peacebuilding, reconciliation, and embracing difference emerge. The wide range of case studies and disciplinary approaches from the MENA region in this volume discusses these issues as the significance of the relationship between local peacebuilding and community development and the impact of youths' civic engagement and local peacebuilding on development and change processes should be considered (McEvoy-Levy, 2006; Ozerdem and Podder, 2015).

To what extent have young people's leadership of CSOs contributed to new structures of civil society? The complications of the relationship between local leadership and the "elite" of national movements and their impact on grassroots participation in the processes of decision-making and development of their society are discussed in this book. These problems have already imposed serious challenges on today's youth, including for young women's engagement, contributions to peacebuilding, and post-conflict processes. The role of youths in peacebuilding is now being introduced; Ozerdem and Podder (2015) discuss youths in conflict and peacebuilding theoretically by highlighting the ways in which they are overlooked in peacebuilding and considering their agential capacity to contribute. This volume presents young people's engagement with a wide range of examples from MENA countries. Alarabeed, for instance, discusses the challenges facing young people's engagement in the post-conflict reconstruction process in the Gaza Strip in Chapter 9.

McEvoy-Levy (2006) has also discussed the foundations of this space and to peacebuilding in *Troublemakers or Peacemakers: Youth and Post-Accord Peacebuilding*. Local peacebuilding, however, has been a significant matter for youths' civic engagement and active participation in contributing to the development and change processes of their societies. Young people are an important part of society, having a considerable impact and influence both in times of peace and conflict, yet they are not included in decision-making processes, community development, or peacebuilding programmes, as Alkahlout discusses in Chapter 2. CSOs play this significant role of engaging the youth in local peacebuilding initiatives. Many CSOs have also held a number of meetings and discussions with representatives of target groups in order to design programmes for young people's engagement in community peace actions (Natil, 2014, 2019, 2020b). Previously, Michels and de Graaf (2010) have discussed the importance of networks of civic engagement to make citizens more qualified.

However, Raweh, in Chapter 8, argues that as long as the peace process in Yemen does not fully include all segments of Yemeni society – the youth in particular, who are the future of the country – then this process will surely be fragile, and violence is likely to break out again in the future. Yemeni youth are at the core of ending their nation's conflict and bringing about peace, yet they are being side-lined from the official negotiations that the UN Office of the Special Envoy of the Secretary-General for Yemen (OSESGY) is conducting.

Meanwhile, some CSOs are trying to engage young women via a participatory approach, which combines discussions, dialogue, coalition-building, interviews, and various interactions between young people themselves and other stakeholders. This includes promoting the level of culture and education for civil society activists (Paffenholz and Spurk, 2010, p. 67). To what extent has women's engagement in grassroots peacebuilding increased their participation in decision-making processes? This explains how they contribute to grassroots and local peacebuilding activities to change their circumstances. Vulnerable and grassroots groups, and women in particular, are still neglected and excluded from community development and democratic participation, including peacebuilding, in formal institutional processes. Their active, profound contributions and multifaceted engagement have been largely invisible in peace processes even after UNSCR 1325, and "usually are informal, ad hoc, and rarely part of formal peace processes, so their stories often drift, unacknowledged" (Porter, 2007, p. 2).

Merrill (2017, p. 124) argues that Arab societies, however, have common values of conservatism, and religion remains an influential factor of both their cultures and behaviours. In many countries, religion is dominant, although some CSOs have invited open-minded religious leaders to deliver statements and lectures to endorse their operations and values of women's active participation in community development and political structures (Merrill, 2017, p. 124). In Chapter 7, Abdo, Abohajeb, and Mohsen discuss the question of whether the direct participation of women in violent conflict is considered as a breakaway from established and imposed local social norms or whether it can be conceived as an emergent conflict-specific tradition. Young people, however, may employ education tools and approaches to increase peacebuilding, just as a specialist/leader employs active listening and mediation to solve family and social problems and civil society activists engage in community development and human rights programmes, employing a community participatory approach to contribute to grassroots peacebuilding (Natil, 2020b). These examples of female community peace-builders' challenges and achievements introduce the grassroots approach of civil society peacebuilding, rather than that of formal state institutions. It discusses the active and influential role of young women in a bottom-up process rather than a top-down approach through formal state institutions (Noma, Aker, and Freeman, 2012, pp. 7–32).

Women's involvement in community activities is a core principle of conflict resolution and community peacebuilding approaches, which also promote dialogue and other peacebuilding mechanisms and tools, as Arostegui (2013) argues:

> [W]omen's empowerment has come with the education, advocacy, and organisational skills that they developed as a result of conflict – they now have women's networks and women's peace groups, which were not there previously.

The process of engagement, however, is challenged by domestic and political violence against women. Chapter 7 also analyses this as a major challenge for civic engagement and social empowerment in a participatory process. The gender issue should, however, be given a specific space to distinguish contributions to conflict and peacebuilding, such as when Pruitt and Lee-Koo (2020) introduced young women and leadership in peace and security. However, women's groups/CSOs have already employed a number of accommodating policies and operations to increase their interventions as discussed in Chapter 7. However, the question of accepting child soldiers in the post-conflict phase remains a precondition for the success of the process of peace resolutions, as Hasona discusses in Chapter 6. Hasona argues that the restorative justice approach is an effective way to assist communities in accepting, understanding, and forgiving child soldiers without stigmatization or rejection. The promotion of justice is an essential approach for the empowerment of youth engagement and their contribution to their communities, as Raweh discusses in Chapter 8. However, excluding young Yemeni people from active engagement in the peace process is a real challenge.

Prospects and challenges for community development

The failure of governments to provide quality services for young people and/or engage them effectively in a transparent policymaking process has already led to widespread discontent among youths, as the UN Youth World Report (2016, p. 14) discusses. Repressive regimes, however, have been found to control young people and their CSOs by dominating financial channels (Weeden, 2015). Natil (2019, 2020a) has previously discussed the barriers facing civil society and its ability to cope with and operate within shifting conditions and restrictive political environments, despite the complexity of the sociocultural and economic context. Occupying the ground between business and government, the youth CSO sector faces a number of regulatory and financial challenges that affect its overall health, legitimacy, and sustainability (Natil, 2020a).

However, violence represents a major challenge to young people's participatory engagement at the grassroots level and to their contributions to the development of their society. Case studies of actual youths who are engaged in community development and peacebuilding should be presented with the aim of presenting real-life experiences. This question has always been an issue in countries that have been shattered by conflict and poverty, such as Yemen, Palestine, and Syria. This book addresses a significant issue of youth engagement and how it can be enhanced by giving young people recommendations and aspirations. In Chapter 8, Raweh investigates what the current main role of the youth is in peacebuilding and how the UNSCR 2250 contributes to enhancing youth participation in peacebuilding in Yemen. However, youth engagement and involvement can also be negative, such as in their radicalism and extremism, as Awan (2016) argues.

The CSOs' activities include helping to eliminate the phenomenon of domestic violence against women in the MENA region. The young women of Yemen, for example, have been subject to different types of violence, owing to the ongoing conflict, divisions, and the social context. Marginalized and vulnerable groups face violence as a serious threat to both their civic engagement and community participation. This represents a major challenge for their integration, advancement, and engagement in the development of their societies. It is used against women and is a consequence of the unequal power relations within the family specifically and in society in general (Jad, 2007, 2018). Müller and Tranchant (2017) write that violence against women can take various forms such as psychological violence, cursing, insults, yelling, and screaming. A UN Women study found in 2017 that 80% of men and 48% of women believe that men should be the decision-makers at home (UN Women and Promundo USA, 2017).

Michels and de Graaf (2010), however, argue that citizen participation is usually considered as a significant aspect of democracy and has positive effects on the quality of democracy. Young people's active participation can be seen as an outcome of their empowerment according to the cultural context of their society (Natil, 2016). Women are often described as victims and marginalized from leading formal political and institutional processes, but they are powerful agents for community peacebuilding education in contexts of conflict (Arostegui, 2013). Women, Potter (2008) writes, have long been distinguished at the forefront of peacebuilding efforts. Their engagement in grassroots peacebuilding is much more visible while men take part in formal political processes. Women's integration into all peacebuilding, therefore, is very important in reconstruction and rebuilding processes following periods of conflict (Potter, 2008, pp. 142–143). Abdo, Abohajeb, and Mohsen present the Yemeni conflict in Chapter 7, which has left an impact on different aspects of Yemeni society. It also assigned new roles to women in response to new developments, thus allowing new players (e.g., Houthi women) to dominate other women in the country. Noma, Aker, and Freeman (2012) discuss the importance of women's voices to breaking cycles of conflict and deepening the concept of peacebuilding. Sharing information about their achievements and challenges in peacebuilding at the grassroots, national, and international levels in contexts of conflict is relevant to women's social and political empowerment and civil society engagement, as Porter discusses (2007).

It is necessary to transfer the pulse of grassroots activism to promote reconciliation and to broadcast positive statements rather than incitements and negativity, as well as to ensure the validity of news before its publication, in order to refute anything that could disturb community peacebuilding initiatives. Women are still fighting to improve their position and to move from the margins of society to become key decision-makers in civil, political, and community work. Their various missions aim for women's civil rights, public freedoms, and contributions to society – despite living in contexts of conflict. Women's leaders are also still attempting to challenge and change the circumstances and constraints that have already placed women in a worse situation than men (Natil, 2019, 2020b).

References

Alkatary, R. (2014, October 15). *The Role of Media in Promoting Community-based Peace*. Working Paper, Culture of Community Peace and Rule of Law Conference, Society Voice Foundation, Gaza City.

Aragones, E. and Sánchez-Pagés, S. (2009). A theory of participatory democracy based on the real case of Porto Alegre. *European Economic Review*, 53(1), 56–72.

Arostegui, J. (2013). Gender, conflict, and peace-building: how conflict can catalyse positive change for women. *Gender & Development*, 21(3), 533–549. doi:10.10 80/13552074.2013.846624.

Awan, A. (2016). Negative youth engagement: involvement in radicalism and extremism. In *Youth Civic Engagement, United Nations World Youth Report*. Accessed on January 13, 2021 https://www.un.org/development/desa/youth /wp-content/uploads/sites/21/2018/12/un_world_youth_report_youth_civic _engagement.pdf.

Berents, B. and McEvoy-Levy, S. (2015). Theorising youth and everyday peace(building), Peacebuilding, *3*(2), 115–125. DOI: 10.1080/21647259.2015.1052627.

Bherer, L., Dufour, P., and Montambeault, F. (2016). The participatory democracy turn: an introduction. *Journal of Civil Society*, *12*(3), 225–230. doi:10.1080/174 48689.2016.1216383.

Cho, A., Byrne, J., and Pelter, Z. (2020). Digital civic engagement by young people. UNICEF Offices of Global insight and Policy. Accessed on January 5, 2021 https://www.unicef.org/sites/default/files/2020-07/Digital-civic-engagement-by -young-people-2020_4.pdf.

CIVICUS (2020). State of Civil Society Report 2020. Accessed on January 14, 2021 https://www.civicus.org/documents/reports-and-publications/SOCS/2020/ SOCS2020_Executive_Summary_en.pdf.

Habermas, J. (1991). *Theory and Practice*. Translated by John Viertel. Cambridge, MA: Beacon Press.

Habermas, J. (1996). *Between Facts and Norms: Contributions to a Discourse Theory of Law and Democracy*. Cambridge, MA: MIT Press.

Hilmer, J. (2010). The state of participatory democratic theory. *New Political Science*, *32*(1), 43–63. DOI: 10.1080/07393140903492118.

Honwana, A. (2013). *Youth and Revolution in Tunisia*. London, New York: Zed Books.

Jad, I. (2007). NGOs: Between buzzwords and social movements. *Development in Practice*, *17*(4–5), 622–629. Doi:10.1080/09614520701469781.

Jad, I. (2018). *The Palestinian women's activism: Nationalism, secularism and Islamism*. New York, NY: Syracuse University Press.

McEvoy-Levy, S. (2006). *Troublemakers or Peacemakers: Youth and Post-Accord Peacebuilding*. University of Notre Dame Press.

Merrill, R. C. (2017). The Middle Eastern gender gap: the state of female political participation before, during and after the 'Arab Spring'. In C. Çakmak (Ed.), *The Arab Spring, Civil Society, and Innovative Activism* (pp. 121–140). London: Palgrave Macmillan Publishers Ltd.

Michels, A. and de Graaf, L. (2010). Examining citizen participation: Local participatory policy making and democracy. *Local Government Studies*, *36*(4), 477–491. DOI:10.1080/03003930.2010.494101.

Müller, C. and Tranchant, J. (2017). International Institute for Environment and Development. Accessed on June 4, 2020 Retrieved from https://www.jstor.org /stable/resrep02733.

Mullard, S. and Aarvik, p. (2020). Supporting civil society during the Covid-19 pandemic. CMI CHR. Michelsen Institute. Accessed on July 25, 2020. https:// www.u4.no/publications/supporting-civil-society-during-the-covid-19-pandemic.pdf.

Natil, I. (2014). A shifting political landscape: NGOs' civic activism and response in the Gaza Strip, 1967–2014. *Journal of Peacebuilding & Development*, *9*(3), 82–87. DOI:10.1080/15423166.2014.983369.

Natil, I. (2016). The challenges and opportunities of donor-driven aid to youth refugees in Palestine. *Journal of Peacebuilding & Development*, *11*(2), 78–82. DOI:10.1080/15423166.2016.1197791.

Natil, I. (2019). The power of civil society: Young leaders' engagement in non-violent actions in Palestine. In I. Natil, C. Pieroban, and L. Tauber (Eds), *The Power of Civil Society in the Middle East and North Africa: Peacebuilding, Change and Development* (pp. 24–36). New York, NY: Routledge.

Natil, I. (2020a). Introducing barriers to effective civil society organisations. In I. Natil, V. Malila, and Y. Sai (Eds), *Barriers to Effective Civil Society Organisations: Political, Social and Financial Shifts* (pp. 9–17). New York, NY: Routledge.

Natil, I. (2020b). Women's community peacebuilding in the occupied Palestinian territories (OPT). In O. Richmond and G. Visoka (Eds), *The Palgrave Encyclopedia of Peace and Conflict Studies* (pp. 1–12). Cham: Palgrave Macmillan. https://doi.org/10.1007/978-3-030-11795-5_47-1.

Noma, E., Aker, D., and Freeman, J. (2012). Heeding women's voices: breaking cycles of conflict and deepening the concept of peacebuilding. *Journal of Peacebuilding & Development*, 7(1), 7–32. DOI:10.1080/15423166.2012.719384.

Ozerdem, A. and S. Podder. (2015). *Youth in Conflict and Peacebuilding*. New York: Palgrave.

Paffenholz, T. (2010). *Civil Society & Peacebuilding: A Critical Assessment*. Boulder, CO: Lynne Rienner.

Paffenholz, T. and Spurk, C. (2010). A comprehensive analytical framework. In T. Paffenholz (Ed.), *Civil Society & Peacebuilding: A Critical Assessment* (pp. 65–75). Boulder, CO: Lynne Rienner.

Peters, K. and El Taraboulsi-McCarthy, Sh. (2020). OPINION: Dealing with COVID-19 in conflict zones needs a different approach. Thomson Reuters Foundation. Accessed on July 24, 2020 https://news.trust.org/item/20200329200250-bj72i/.

Polletta, F. (2016). Participatory enthusiasms: A recent history of citizen engagement initiatives. *Journal of Civil Society*, 12(3), 231–246. DOI:10.1080/17448689.2016.1213505.

Porter, E. (2007). *Peacebuilding: Women in International Perspective*. London: Routledge.

Porter, E. (2013). Rethinking women's empowerment. *Journal of Peacebuilding & Development*, 8(1), 1–14. DOI:10.1080/15423166.2013.785657.

Potter, M. (2008). Women, civil society and peace-building in Northern Ireland: Paths to peace through women's empowerment. In Christopher Farrington (Ed), *Global Change, Civil Society and the Northern Ireland Peace Process Implementing the Political Settlement*, UK: Palgrave Macmillan.

Pruitt, L. and K. Lee-Koo (2020). *Young Women and Leadership*. London: Routledge.

Spurk, C. (2010). Understanding civil society. In T. Paffenholz (Ed.), *Civil Society and Peacebuilding: A Critical Assessment* (pp. 3–26). Boulder, CO: Lynne Rienner.

UN Women and Promundo USA. (2017). Understanding masculinities: International Men and Gender Equality Survey (IMAGES) – Middle East and North Africa, Egypt, Lebanon, Morocco, and Palestine. Accessed on June 9, 2020 Retrieved from https://promundoglobal.org/wp-content/uploads/2017/05/IMAGES-MENA-Multi-Country-Report-EN-16May2017-web.pdf.

UNICEF (2020). Youth led initiative fund launched on international volunteering day. a new youth led initiative fund to support volunteering. Press Release.

Accessed on January 4, 2021 https://www.unicef.org/jordan/press-releases/youth-led-initiative-fund-launched-international-volunteering-day.

Weeden, L. (2015). Abandoning "legitimacy": reflections on Syria and Yemen. In Hudson, M. (Ed.), *The Crisis of the Arab State: Study Group Report*. Cambridge, MA: Harvard Kennedy School: Middle East Initiative.

Youngs, R. and Panchulidze, E. (2020). *Global Democracy & COVID-19: Upgrading International Support*, (Co publishers) European Endowment for Democracy, The Carter Center, European Partnership for Democracy, European Network of Political Foundations, IFES, IRI, NDI, NED, Parliamentary Centre, and WFD. Accessed on July 26, 2020 https://www.idea.int/sites/default/files/publications/global-democracy-and-covid-19.pdf.

2 Youth engagement in local peacebuilding in the Gaza Strip

Ola Alkahlout

Introduction

The Palestinian internal conflict between Hamas and Fatah in 2006 resulted in over 300 Palestinian deaths in the Gaza Strip and the West Bank (Saleh, 2007). The consequences of this conflict resulted in an internal division in the Gaza Strip, as well as widespread poverty, unemployment, displacement, and loss of social stability. The area is still classified as "volatile:" no genuine settlement has been reached, as many endeavours to bring about a peace agreement have been in vain. The youth (aged 15–29) form approximately 30% of the population (PASSIA, 2017) in the Strip. Young people are therefore regarded as a major part of society, with considerable impact and influence on their societies in times of peace and in conflict. The potential for local peacebuilding is possible by engaging the youth in decision-making. This age group is the most affected by the internal conflict but can also be the most active agent for any proposed reconciliation initiative.

Palestinians have been living under one of the most protracted conflicts in modern history. Following the Arab-Israeli war of 1948, the Gaza Strip was under Egyptian administration until its occupation by the Israeli army during the 1967 Six-Day War (Fisher and Wicker, 2010; UNRWA, 2014). The conflict between the Israelis and the Palestinians intensified with the first *intifada* (uprising) between 1987 and 1993, and the second *Intifada* between 2000 and 2005, resulting in 5,616 Palestinians being killed (Peters and Newman, 2013; Al-Jazeera, 2016). The *intifada* was a protest against Israeli repression including "beatings, shootings, killings, house demolitions, uprooting of trees, deportations, extended imprisonments, and detentions without trial" (Ackerman and DuVall, 2000, pp. 401–407). The Gaza-Jericho agreement between the Palestinian Liberation Organization (PLO) and Israel was established on May 4, 1994: Israel's governance over the Gaza Strip would be transferred to the new Palestinian self-rule authority, the PNA (Fisher and Wicker, 2010; UNRWA 2014).

The reconstruction of Gaza primarily began through a multi-level mechanism involving international, national, government, and non-governmental organizations (NGOs) (United Nations, 2014). The Gaza Strip began to improve on the socio-economic level, shown through the permanent opening of schools, the building of hospitals, airports, and seaports, and less restrictive travelling regulations. Gaza began to emerge as a city which could sustain itself and prosper, in spite of the extraordinary challenges it faced. According to Abolkomsan (2005), the Palestinian economy was marked by a notable development, as the output increased by 12.2% in the Gaza Strip in 1998. The GDP in real terms in 1998 was about 18%. This reflected the growth in the amount of foreign income and financial assistance, as the volume of international aid increased from US$419 million in 1998 to US$482 million in 1999, while the unemployment rate decreased from 11.8% in the same year to 10% in 1999 (Abolkomsan, 2005).

Israel continued to maintain its full control over the region. Hamas, the Islamist movement in the Gaza Strip and the West Bank secured a decisive victory over Fatah in the 2006 elections (Roy, 2013). Israel consequently imposed a blockade on Gaza shortly after this victory, denouncing Hamas as a "terrorist" organization (Milton-Edwards and Farrell, 2010; Al-Jazeera, 2017). Israel continued with its attacks on the Gaza Strip from 2008–2019 through air, land, and sea military raids, resulting in 4,979 Gazan fatalities and 233 Israeli fatalities (OCHA, 2019b). The Israeli government had also imposed a blockade on all Gaza Strip fronts. The blockade confined up to two million Gazans in the third most densely populated area in the world (PCBS, 2015; UNRWA, 2019). The Palestinian political divide, and the prolonged closure of the Rafah Border Crossing with Egypt, continued (and continues) to hamper economic and social development (UNDP, 2016).

Only one in eight college-educated Palestinians could find degree-related work during the *intifada* (Ackerman and DuVall, 2000. pp. 401–407). Poverty and child labour, for example, have exceeded 80% (MEMO, 2019); about 68% of households in Gaza experience moderate to severe levels of food shortages, and the unemployment rate increased from 44% in 2017 to 52% in 2018 (OCHA, 2019a). The history of conflict, whether internal (Hamas and Fatah) or external (Palestine and Israel), has played a major part in Gaza's current situation and on the lives of young people there.

The conflict between Hamas: its effects on the Gazan youth

Fatah and Hamas, established in 1957 and 1987, respectively, are two of the most popular factions in Palestine; others include the Islamic *Jihad* movement and The Popular Front for the Liberation of Palestine (Zuhur,

2008). The conflict between Hamas and Fatah was little known internationally until after the 2006 and 2007 events (Human Rights Watch, 2008). The Palestinian division which occurred in June 2007 affected all aspects of Palestinian society. Disputes within families occurred. These were characterized by political and factional tensions, often leading to estrangement. Close connections were no longer protected by the freedom of opinion; the mere expression of a differing thought could cause dissension (Auda, 2011). The social impact of the internal conflict remains to this day. The state of frustration and deterioration has also found resonance through interviews with the youth. Jamal (neutral) pointed out the tragic situation in Gaza.

> Our cause has seen, in the past decades, the worst stages, and lost a lot of those who supported it and [believed in] its justice. Our people have turned from a revolutionary people who dream of liberation, to [an] exhausted society of a hungry revolution, maximising their aspirations and hopes for a living, and a loaf of bread. We see [this] only through the parties in the conflict, and [it] only reaches their supporters and their followers; as for the citizen, he "died," and no longer makes a sound with the army of graduates without any ambition or even hope for life and optimism for the future.

When one is exposed to a state of desperation and lack of basic human needs, the struggle to survive supersedes secondary issues such as the political situation in Palestine. The split between Hamas and Fatah is not only between the leaders, it is also present amongst the Gazans themselves. The relationship between Gazans and political parties is based on party affiliation (Auda, 2011). The respondents recognized the 2007 conflict from a factional perspective. Karim (Fateh member) said: "Yes, I am aware that, somebody hid in the name of Islam, and used it to foster a spirit of division and bloodshed to reach power and control the money." Doaa' (Hamas member) on the other hand, declared: "Yes, I am aware of what happened, and I can explain it by the oppression of Fatah and its corruption, which eventually led to armed fighting to purge the Strip of [Fatah's] treachery." The youth are conscious of the circumstances according to the views of their parties. The volatile political environment and outlook have remained unchanged since 2007, and internal conflict could be reignited. There have been many attempts at reconciliation between Hamas and Fatah, such as Qatar's peacemaking efforts between the two parties in 2017, with little success (AIJAC, 2012; Majed, 2017). To prevent such a conflict and its disastrous impacts, local peacebuilding initiatives involving the youth have become fundamental.

Youth: a potential resource for peacebuilding initiatives

Peacebuilding is defined as "removal of causes of wars and offer[s] alternatives to war in situations where wars might occur" (Galtung, 1976. pp. 297–298). Brahimi further clarifies that, peacebuilding is a set of "activities undertaken on the far side of conflict to reassemble the foundations of peace and provide the tools for building on those foundations, something that is more than just the absence of war" (United Nations Peacebuilding, 2010, p. 5). Local peacebuilding is defined as "actions initiated, led, and implemented by people in and from their own context, both at the grassroots and nationally – [local peacebuilding] is therefore essential" (Peace Direct, 2019).

The youth in Gaza Strip are a valuable asset to local peacebuilding initiatives, despite the devastating results of their involvement in the conflicts in Gaza. They have the potential to make a difference by engaging in local peacebuilding initiatives, if they were offered the opportunity. A number of interviewees were not optimistic about the possibility of achieving local peace. They blamed the leaders of Hamas and Fatah as the main decision-makers for the lack of reconciliation efforts. Muhammad (neutral) said: "Youth [political] parties are difficult to reconcile because each party adheres to its views," The majority of interviewees, however, were optimistic about the local peace process through the youth in Gaza. Ahmed (Hamas member) said: "Yes, if the parties [would] reconcile with each other, [this would lead] to change in society for the better, and reach the [desired] goals." Jamal (neutral) added: "Youth parties are reconciled with each other, and any naïve disagreement that hinders this reconciliation and cohesion can be completely overcome."

The Gazan youth are optimistic and persistent in their desire for reconciliation between Hamas and Fatah. Their potential, they believe, lies in the large percentage of youth in the Gazan population. This underutilized resource could greatly influence decision-making to achieve conflict resolution. Gazan youth's optimism is not only based on a better future, it also promotes sharing awareness, and the convergence of views. The majority of respondents believed that engaging the youth in local peacebuilding initiatives would not only provide jobs and a livelihood but is among the most important methods that would contribute to achieving local peace between the conflicting political parties. The contribution CSOs would make through engagement of the youth in peacebuilding initiatives in Gaza would help Gaza achieve local peace.

Gazan CSOs and local peacebuilding

Gaza's political situation in terms of external and internal conflicts has made it a typical fertile ground for CSO activity. The Gaza Strip receives significant aid and financial support from Qatar, for example. Qatar's recent financial support reached US$30 million, regardless of the controversies associated with Qatar's humanitarian aid's alleged intentions (Alkahlout, 2020). CSOs have the expertise to raise awareness of problems arising in affected areas through publications and community workshops to minimize the damage caused by the conflicts. This was confirmed by the *International Platform of NGOs Working For Palestine study* 2019: the number of Palestinian CSOs reached 4,616 (42%) in the West Bank, and 31% in the Gaza Strip (ipalestine, 2019). The study showed that, due to the blockade imposed on Gaza, it had created challenges which stood in the way of CSO relief and charitable work, while marginalizing other sectors which are important in terms of local development. The interest due on aid also significantly overwhelmed CSO financial resources – mainly for relief programmes – as a result of the escalating crisis in the living conditions of the cities besieged or destroyed by the wars. The extensive restrictions imposed by the Israeli authorities or the PNA on the movement of money into Gaza, and access to these organizations impeded their operations (ipalestine, 2019).

CSOs provide services such as health and education, rehabilitation for the disabled, housing, and economic development. A USAID (2013) report explains that CSOs in Gaza now lead immediate humanitarian relief and other urgent needs, rather than planning and designing community services or long-term objectives. The blockade of Gaza was not the only challenge CSOs faced. The internal conflict between Hamas and Fatah has also tightened the screws on freedom of expression in CSO work, according to CSO employees. The question of whether an organization is affiliated to Hamas or Fatah disturbed the interview respondents. CSO's apparent lack of transparency and professional integrity was a major concern. Muhammad (neutral) explained: "Of course [the youth] do not have [any] confidence in CSOs, because all institutions work for their own benefit [to avoid bankruptcy] or [closure] in light of the blockade." Saber (organization staff member) confirmed this: "Not all projects [are jointly operated]. There are projects which [are made] specific[ally] for the youth of the same faction, and a few of those [apply] to the Gazan citizen." The respondents' opinions were divided regarding the local institutions having an active role in family dissention and conflict prevention. Rasha (organization staff member) said: "Most Palestinian institutions and organizations in the sector are politicized or operate within the terms of the funder […] some are positive, and some fuel the Palestinian division." Abdu Allah (organization staff member) disagreed: "They played a role in calling for reconciliation and reducing the gap between the Hamas and Fatah movements."

CSOs' lack of transparency, on the other hand, fuels the conflict between Hamas and Fatah followers. This was evident in Muhammad's and Rasha's responses that CSOs in Gaza have a dual role: encouraging the factional division on one hand and reducing the gap between the Palestinian factions on the other. The majority of the CSO respondents, or those affiliated with the two factions, stressed that this did not eliminate the role of CSOs allied to each faction from the importance of supporting projects which could serve the local peace process. The harsh criticism of the CSO in Gaza was unanimous; however, most of the respondents were also optimistic about the positive role the youth could play towards resolving the internal conflict between Hamas and Fatah. According to Peace Direct (2019) local organizations have an important role in achieving local peacebuilding in the region. These organizations could address several improvements: simplify grant allocation and management by applying a stronger focus on mutual trust and collaboration; using adaptive programming, thus lightening the compliance burden on both parties by adopting a greater tolerance of risk; tailoring programme design and grant application processes for local initiatives; designing strategies and programmes to be more inclusive of local voices and actions; and finally, reflecting on their roles and priorities.

The most supported projects were political awareness, convergence of views between the youth of Hamas and Fatah, and improved living and economic conditions through job opportunities in peacebuilding initiatives. Two projects were proposed by the respondents: spreading awareness and convergence of opinions, and initiatives to improve living and economic conditions. If these could be achieved, they would contribute to attaining local peacebuilding and reconciliation of the internal conflict between Hamas and Fatah in Gaza.

Spreading awareness and convergence of views through local peacebuilding initiatives

Raising awareness of the current events in the conflict between Hamas and Fatah is considered to be an important step towards resolving the tensions between the two parties. Understanding each party's views and reaching an agreement – or at least a compromise – would go a long way towards avoiding the recurrence of the events of 2006–2007. Gazan CSO staff agreed and were keen to support awareness projects between Hamas and Fatah. Abdu Allah and Muhammad, members of staff organizations, agreed that: "The role of NGOs is currently limited to fostering dialogue – raising citizens' awareness of dialogue and tolerance." Muhammad added: Dialogue and tolerance can be achieved "through legal awareness and promotion of a culture of human rights in society." Awareness projects could be successful in peacebuilding, with the cooperation of the youth movement in Gaza. This is in line with the study by Peace Direct (2019) which reported considerable success in three stages of impact.

First stage: preventing, reducing, or stopping violence; improved optimism regarding knowledge of peaceful approaches in addressing conflict opinion-formers to better understand how their words can shape peace or conflict. Early warning and response mechanisms help to avoid violence by engaging with aware and informed youth, thus making them less vulnerable to recruitment to violence. The CSOs in Gaza propose separate youth projects for each of the followers of Hamas and Fatah. Dialogue between the two parties' followers is one of the key elements towards local peacebuilding; monitoring the words which fuel the conflict, is another. Hamas accuses Fatah members of stealing donation money, for instance, and Fatah accuses Hamas members of using Islam to hide behind its persecution and violence, according to Karim and Doaa'. This calls for project trainers to act as mediators between the two factions. The mediators are usually national or religious representatives of Gazan society who are respected by both parties, or they are trusted international mediators. Individual training projects will prepare the followers of each faction to move to the second stage: consensus.

Consensus has two dimensions: horizontal and vertical relationships. Horizontal relationships (equal standing) help to improve relationships between and among people and "others." Improved empathy for the views and problems faced by "others," and increased trust, tolerance, and forgiveness are the first steps towards agreement. Improved understanding of the underlying reasons for the conflict and proactive peace initiatives by ethnic, religious, and community leaders to develop ties and cohesion, is another step. Building practical links and better relations with "other" groups will develop into mutual support. The two factions will meet through joint projects on awareness-raising in the convergence of views, and distance themselves from the points that fuel the dispute. The challenge which hinders these two proposals is the lack of communication between the youth and leaders of each party. Improved or improving relationships between people and those who govern them (vertical relationships) is the second dimension of consensus, and the third stage.

Vertical relationships (top-down) help to improve a better understanding between those with authority and power and citizens, and calls for practical collaboration such as dialogue regarding conflict issues (Peace Direct, 2019). The new governance approaches towards conflict resolution, policies adopted by communities, and local and national government community-based peace initiatives integrate women, young people, and minorities into decision-making. Political and community leaders, celebrities, dignitaries, and so on, have also had an active role in reconciliation between different parties in conflict zones. Interpeace (2017) has identified three tracks showing the levels of influence and formal organization of the actors in peacebuilding: (i) political elites and decision-makers; (ii) civil society and local government; and (iii) local communities and individuals within the broader population. A single-track approach is unlikely to solve the internal conflict between the factions. The leaders of Hamas and Fatah (Track 1) cannot agree to any deals without educating their followers about what these agreements stipulate. The youth are the ones who will coexist, implement, and practise these agreements; unsuitable agreements will undoubtedly be challenged. Jamal (neutral) says: "The youth parties are reconciled with each other, […] but, the youth parties [question] the credibility of Hamas and Fatah in resolving the dispute."

The project goals for the youth of Gaza (Track 3) cannot be achieved in the convergence of views, except through contact with leaders. This calls for the mediators (Track 2) in the rapprochement between the leaders and the followers. CSO-funded projects would bring together the two parties with the mediators' support. It should be noted here that reconciliation does not take place between Hamas and Fatah. The central authority is Hamas in Gaza, and Fatah in the West Bank. Reference by each leadership to the other, seldom (if ever) occurs.

Challenges to achieving awareness-spreading and convergence of views projects

The projects for achieving the spreading of awareness and convergence of views face three key challenges: omission of followers in decision-making initiatives; repression and brutality of Hamas and Fatah on the opposition's followers; and the weak relationship between the leaders of Hamas and Fatah in Gaza Strip and the West Bank. The omission of followers, especially the youth, in crucial decision-making regarding the Palestinian issue or reconciliation between Hamas and Fatah remains problematic. Peace Direct (2019) says, local peacebuilders are too often starved of support by their political leaders, meaning international help is crucial. International donors and organizations, however, are often unwilling or unable to step into the argument. According to the respondents in this research in the Gaza Strip (2020), where politicians or leaders from Hamas or Fatah intervene in the fateful decisions of Gazan youth, no consultation with the youth is conducted. Youth involvement is a pivotal aspect of local ownership.

A study by Interpeace (2017, p. 5) discovered that, "Youth as well as development specialists and academics, emphasize that young people are absent from the processes of decision-making, community development, and participation in building peace and achieving security." Gazan youth possess a marginal role in decision-making regarding their short- or long-term future. This concern was expressed by the respondents to the question: *Do you believe that today's youth in Gaza possesses a voice regarding the conflict between Hamas and Fatah in Gaza?* There were many respondents who agreed with the notion that, the youth's attitudes and opinions were suppressed, and could not reach those in political power – Hamas or Fatah. Khaled (Hamas supporter) said: "Most of the time, the youth's voice is weak, not supported, and means little to those in power." Karim (Fateh supporter), added: "They have a strong voice outside of Gaza because conversation regarding the end of division in Palestine through the termination of the leadership of the PLO is considered an act of treason." The lack of youth participation has proven to be a considerable obstacle, as it hinders reconciliation efforts. It is not possible to conclude agreements with leaders without referring to the youth, who are at the root of the issue. The method of relaying the youth's voice to leaders could be achieved, either through peaceful demonstrations or social media, was agreed by most of the respondents. Osama (Hamas supporter) suggested creating a youth council which does not belong to any faction or organization, whose approach would support the youth, and their capacity for development. This proposal and others should be taken into consideration. It is the youth of today who will implement and save the deteriorating situation in Gaza; without their involvement, there will be no peace in the region.

The arbitrary acts of repression and brutality by Hamas and Fatah on the opposition followers is another issue. The PNA (Fatah) in the West Bank and Hamas in the Gaza Strip, for instance, have carried out a large number of arbitrary arrests in recent years (Human Rights Watch, 2018), in spite of the peaceful criticism of the authorities on social media – especially by journalists – and independent party members.

Initiatives to improve living and economic conditions

The second suggested initiative is to improve the living conditions of young people, such as creating new job opportunities. Peace cannot be built in a society that is starving and suffering. A research study on the causes and effects of violence on Egyptian society, similar to the Gazan community situation, ascribed the reason for the widening circle of violence within Arab families to the increase in economic pressures due to unemployment and low family incomes. This leads to "psychological pressure" (Khader et al. 2008–2009, p. 16). Despite the effort to support projects in which CSOs contribute to Gazan society such as recreational trips, aid, awareness sessions for young people – festivals and photo exhibitions – education for the youth – security awareness sessions on the occupation through summer camps, and so on, were of little help. They did not contribute to improving the living conditions of young people. The financial and in-kind assistance from the international community given to Gaza cannot be denied or ignored, but its lack of contact on the ground is due to both internal and external challenges.

Conclusion

The possible prevention of the recurrence of the 2006–2007 internal conflict between Hamas and Fatah in the Gaza Strip can be achieved through local peacebuilding. The positive impact young people's civic engagement and local peacebuilding abilities would have in community development is evident. Considerable significance has been given to the Gazan youth as they constitute one-third of the population of Gaza. CSOs also play an important role in supporting projects in the peacebuilding sector. The youth's potential lies in their optimism, persistence, and high percentage of the population. These aspects could be driving factors in the influence of decision-making to achieve conflict resolutions. The conflict environment has provided an ideal opportunity for the work of CSOs, yet simultaneously, their work has been hindered by such conflicts.

The CSOs' work in Gaza has been well received by the international community due to their provision of services in health, education, housing, and so on. This was not a smooth and swift process, however, due, in part, to party-political affiliations, poor professional practices, and most importantly, the blockade on Gaza. The inefficiency of CSOs was shown through the bias in the distribution of aid, confirmed by some of the respondents. Two projects were proposed by the youth to achieve local peacebuilding: spreading awareness and convergence of views, and initiatives to improve living and economic conditions. The possibilities and challenges of achieving each initiative in local peacebuilding remain in the balance. The lack of communication between leaders and followers in raising awareness and being informed of developments in the conflict is a significant barrier to achieving peace. The arbitrary acts of repression and brutality by both Hamas and Fatah on the opposition followers is another obstacle to peace.

References

Abolkomsan, Kh. (2005). 'An Analytical Study of the Reality of the Palestinian Economy: Between Investment Opportunities and Future Challenges'. Accessed October 31, 2019 [online] available at https://bit.ly/2XtNBZh.

Ackerman, P. and DuVall, J. (2000). *A Force More Powerful: A Century of Non-violent Conflict*. New York: St. Martin's Press.

Al-Jazeera (2016). 'The Second Palestinian Intifada'. Accessed September 2, 2020 [online] available at https://bit.ly/2YZ7BEm.

Al-Jazeera (2017). 'Milestones of Qatar's Support to the Besieged Gaza Strip'. Accessed November 1, 2019 [online] available at http://bit.ly/34wcvt1.

Alkahlout, O. (2020). *Barriers to Effective Civil Society Organisations: Political, Social and Financial Shifts*. 1st edn Ed. by Natil, I., Malila, V., and Sai, Y. London: Routledge, Taylor & Francis Group. Accessed September 2, 2020 [online] available at https://bit.ly/2wUznal.

Auda, A. (2011). 'The Problematic Relationship Between Fatah and Hamas and its Impact on the Democratic Transformation Process in Palestine (2004–2010)'. Accessed September 2, 2020 [online] available at https://bit.ly/2EVKHqq.

Australia/Israel and Jewish Affairs Council, AIJAC (2012). 'The Latest Fatah-Hamas Agreement in Doha'. Accessed October 31, 2019 [online] available at https://aijac.org.au/update/the-latest-fatah-hamas-agreement-in-doha/.

Fisher, D. and Wicker, B. (Eds) (2010). *Just War on Terror?: A Christian and Muslim Response*. New York: Ashgate.

Galtung, J. (1976). Three Approaches to Peace: Peacekeeping, Peacemaking, and Peacebuilding.' in *Peace, War and Defense: Essays in Peace Research*. Ed. by Galtung, J. Copenhagen: Ejlers.

Human Rights Watch (2008). 'World Report 2008. Events of 2007'. Accessed September 2, 2020 [online] available at https://bit.ly/3bjiyWn.

Human Rights Watch (2018). 'Two Authorities, One Way, Zero Dissent: Arbitrary Arrest and Torture Under the Palestinian Authority and Hamas.' Accessed September 2, 2020 [online] available at https://bit.ly/3lCVBC6.

Interpeace (2017). Track 6: A Strategy for Inclusive Peacebuilding. Accessed December 18, 2017 [online] available at http://bit.ly/38QIAOh.

iPalestine (2019). 'An analytical view of the reality of Palestinian civil society organizations'. Accessed September 2, 2020 [online] available at https://bit.ly/2Z1iN3o.

Khader, Z., Al-Sawy, N., Mohsen, D., and Abd Alhalim, J. (2008–2009). 'The Causes of Violence and its Effects on the Egyptian Society.' Accessed September 2, 2020 [online] available at https://bit.ly/3hSTDLJ.

Majed M. (2017). 'Does "Qatar" Initiative Succeed in Ending the Palestinian Division?' Accessed November 1, 2019 [online] available at http://lnnk.in/tQx.

Middle East Monitor, MEMO (2019). 'Poverty Rate in Gaza Exceeds 80%.' Accessed October 31, 2019 [online] available at https://www.middleeastmonitor.com/20190118-poverty-rate-in-gaza-exceeds-80/.

Milton-Edwards, B. and Farrell, S. (2010). *Hamas: The Islamic Resistance Movement*. Cambridge, UK: Polity.

The Palestinian Academic Society for the Study of International Affairs, PASSIA (2017). 'The Palestinian Youth Generation: Especially in Jerusalem.' Accessed September 2, 2020 [online] available at https://bit.ly/3jIhAWm.

Palestinian Central Bureau of Statics, PCBS (2015). 'Palestinians at the End of 2015.' Accessed October 31, 2019 [online] available from http://bit.ly/2Hvo9e5.

Peace Direct (2019). 'Summary Report: June 2019. Local peacebuilding: What works and why.' Accessed September 2, 2020 [online] available at https://bit.ly /2DaksvX.

Peters, J. and Newman, D. (2013). *The Routledge Handbook on the Israeli-Palestinian Conflict.* London and New York: Routledge.

Roy, S. (2013). 'Hamas and Civil Society in Gaza: Engaging the Islamist Social Sector.' Accessed October 31, 2019 [online] available at http://lnnk.in/rgD.

Saleh, M. (2007). *The Palestinian Strategic Report 2006.* Beirut, Lebanon: Al-Zaytouna Centre for Studies and Consultations.

United Nations Development Program, UNDP (2016). 'Introduction and Context: Challenges to Development in Gaza.' Accessed November 1, 2019 [online] available at http://bit.ly/2WIJWpz.

United Nations Office for the Coordination of Humanitarian Affairs Occupied Palestinian Territories, OCHA (2019a). 'Child Labour Increasing in Gaza.' Accessed October 31, 2019 [online] available at https://www.ochaopt.org/ content/child-labour-increasing-gaza.

United Nations Office for the Coordination of Humanitarian Affairs Occupied Palestinian Territories, OCHA (2019b). 'Data on Casualties & nbsp.' Accessed November 1, 2019 [online] available at http://bit.ly/2Ht047F.

United Nations Peacebuilding (2010). 'UN Peacebuilding: An Orientation.' Accessed August 20, 2017 [online] available at https://bit.ly/3hTW8NQ.

United Nations (2014). 'The Origins of the Palestine Problem and its Development: Part Five (1989–2000).' Accessed September 2, 2020 [online] available at https://bit.ly/3jxjkBY.

United Nations Relief Working Agency for Palestine Refugees in the Near East, UNRWA (2014). '*2014 oPt Emergency Appeal Annual Report (Including the 2014 Gaza Flash Appeal Report.'*. Amman, Jordan: United Nations Relief and Works Agency for Palestine Refugees in the Near East 2015.

United Nations Relief Working Agency, UNRWA (2019). 'Working in the Gaza Strip.' Accessed November 1, 2019 [online] available at http://bit.ly/39Bhg6X.

United States Agency for International Development, USAID (2013). 'CSO Sustainability Report 2013 for the Middle East and North Africa.' Accessed October 31, 2019 [online] available at http://lnnk.in/q8D.

Zuhur, Sh. (2008). 'Hamas and Israel: Conflicting Strategies of Group-Based Politics.' Accessed September 2, 2020 [online] available at https://bit.ly /2QP8E5e.

3 COVID-19, youth, and the engineered social movements in Iran

Nader Ganji, Mohsen Moheimany, and Morvarid Salehi

Introduction

Rulers of Iran have long been attempting to forge a state–society relationship by fostering state-sponsored activism. Nonetheless, it was only after the formation of the Islamic regime in 1979 that the rulers genuinely succeeded in designing, establishing, and developing huge organized civil society institutions by way of youth engagement. The name of the new machinery of the state in Iran was Basij, the largest social enterprise in Iranian history. Such an institution mostly resembles the Society of the 10th of December in France, the members of which overwhelmed the victory of Napoleon in the presidential election 1848. Similar to their Iranian counterparts, this band, as the Emperor's work and very idea, included *lumpenproletariats* and opportunists who were secretly under the control of military leaders (Marx, 1954).

The literature of political science implies macro structure factors, such as shifts in state strategies and ideologies, as well as changes in the arrangement of political opportunities, may affect the status of social movements (Porta and Diani, 1999). In some undemocratic regimes, including Iran, constitutional aspects of democracy, as well as republican institutions, are limitedly integrated into the structure, laws, and policies (Kubba, 2000; Ottaway, 2005; Wigell, 2008). In such a setting, the power of leaders in messing, engineering, and controlling social movements and popular forces is considerable (Hydemann, 2007; Karl, 1995).

As far as the youth movement is concerned, Earl et al. (2017) point to a general move from institutionalized towards non-institutionalized activism. This move includes a transformation of public activism from electoral and party activism towards NGOs, and particularly the youth's move towards short-term activism such as street protests and volunteerism. Some political science scholars state that youth participation is decreasing in some countries (Delli Carpini, 2000). Heydemann (2007, p. 5) discusses the methods

authoritarian leaders used to contain and employ their rising civil societies, which constituted youths, with the purpose of generating "political
resources that bolster regime's hold on power." Such methods are used by
utilizing public resources. A number of studies also discussed the recruitment of social movements through engineering political institutions and
competitions, including manipulating laws and using an ideology to appropriate official and unofficial practices (Liverani, 2008). The patron–client
relationships in neo-patrimonial orders root down into the deep sections
and levels of the government and society by the means of formal and informal rules (Erdmann and Engel, 2006; Lemarchand and Legg, 1972; Muno,
2010).

Using the state apparatus and resources to implant and grow a dependent
civil society is the mechanism of expanding clientelist networks. Thousands
of social groups, as members of these networks, have blossomed across the
Middle East, North Africa, South America, and Eastern Europe with the
legal and financial help of their governments (Heydemann, 2007). Many of
these groups are rent-seekers or state-sponsored insider groups that, while
benefitting from privilege, serve the leaders, either intentionally or unin-
tentionally (Clarke, 1998; Fowler, 1993; Grant, 1989). Then, powerholders
may find an unusual situation appropriate to expand their loyal forces. In
particular, crises and focusing events, as Kingdon (1984) points out, require
rulers' attention and action. This is when the stage is ready for bringing in
loyal groups with the excuse of solving public issues.

History of modern loyalists

In Iran, forming groups loyal to the rulers traces its roots back to almost a
century ago; it was during the Qajar reign (1779–1925), contemporaneously
with the expression of public dissatisfaction especially by means of occupying the streets and running demonstrations against the government. The
government, indeed, was the outcome of an alliance between the Shah and a
number of social strata, such as clergy, merchants, and judges. Nevertheless,
relationships with the West soon undermined this form of government and it
was ultimately crumbled by the waves of the Constitutional Revolution, as a
democratizing movement (1905–1911) (Abrahamian, 1968).

In the midst of the Revolution, however, both a lack of a central government's being capable of intervening and the gradual decreasing power of
the state-provided groups and associations with minimum space for operation (Kazemi, 1996). Protesters relied on the power of streets and therefore,
numerous rallies were organized by the revolutionaries. The court, nonetheless, soon found a way of battling back in the same vein, by mobilizing the
supporters of the Shah, many of whom had been paid to fight the dissidents

on the streets (Poulson, 2006, p. 130). The constitutionalists lost the monopoly of the streets and were seriously challenged on their home ground by the royalists by the end of 1907 (Abrahamian, 1969). Ever since, the crowd has become more important to the Iranian leaders, since a vast loyal band may be useful during times of crisis in challenging the power of dissidents.

During the reign of Reza Shah (1925–1941), state institutions were either formed or totally reconstructed. The voice of dissidents was silenced by a campaign of arrest and intimidation and the legacy of the Revolution was totally ruined. Parties were marginalized or disbanded, elections were strictly controlled by the state, the political sphere was closed, and group activities were prevented (Foran, 1993). Had a protest emerged on the street, the military force would have acted as pro-Shah protesters. Afterwards, though, a new period of political freedom began with the fall of Reza Shah in 1941, following the occupation of the country by the Allies during World War II. In this period, central power became unstable and the struggle between different factions within the government provided political parties and groups with the opportunity of having a public presence (Ghaffary and Azizimehr, 2015). Many politicians were willing to maintain the freedom of the streets, since they were of the opinion that "the suppression of the crowd would result in the re-establishment of court autocracy" (Abrahamian, 1968, p. 210). Even though this was ended by the 1953 coup which resulted in large street demonstrations. Pro-Shah groups occupied the streets and marched through Tehran against Prime Minister Mosaddeq. Royalists, including paid gang leaders, made the coup happen (Lucey, 2019). This came along with the use of violence to impose social control or to achieve mob rule and it was combined with the support of the military (Jahanbegloo, 2013).

During the land reform and profit-sharing projects, which were embarked on in the 1950s, Mohammad Reza Shah (1941–1979) endeavoured to buy the support of farmers and labourers, respectively. Not only did this make these groups, including youth, dissatisfied, but it also disappointed the clerics who had been supported by donations from these groups and were against the modernization process (Wagner, 2010, p. 42). Such projects led to the transformation of the existing factions within the society, most of which were now dissatisfied with their share of capital in the political economy. The Shah established the *Rastakhiz* (Resurrection) party in 1975 in response to such challenges and made it the only legal political party of the country, with compulsory membership. In practice, nonetheless, the party held few organizational events, despite its thousand cells and branches all across the country. Lacking a clear ideology, it was artificially grafted onto the public overnight. It also attacked the bazaar, ran large-scale campaigns, and criticized the clergy (Yom, 2016, p. 142). Thus, whilst it was designed to strengthen the monarchy among the wider Iranian society by establishing institutionalized links between government and people, it ran counter to its initial objective and added to public dissatisfaction in the run-up to the 1979 Revolution (Abrahamian, 2008).

Youth and loyalists under the Islamic regime

The role of the youth grew in importance, especially in the 1979 revolution. Their population had massively increased during the 1970s and they were regarded as the main and the most active force during the revolutionary activities. More than 70% of the population were under 29 (Firouzbakhch, 1988. pp. 94–95). This was the first time that an educated young generation had emerged, with hundreds of thousands of new annual high school graduates and university applicants (Ganji, 2002, p. 5). These combined with numerous students studying abroad who had established the Confederation of Iranian Students, a huge opposition institution which had become as politicized as other opponents since the 1960s (Bayandor, 2019, p. 121). These groups, alongside the rural youth living in the slums of Tehran and the outskirts of other cities searching for jobs, had cultural dislocations, dissatisfactions, and frustrations in common (Ganji, 2002).

Following the revolution, the Islamic camp, as the new rulers, rejected the demands of other revolutionary groups and commenced reconstructing the main pillars of power such as the army (Halliday, 1979). The new regime now had a new privilege: recruiting and mobilizing the politicized masses. For this reason, it widely employed a radical rhetoric directed against foreign actors and internal liberals; a language highly valued in mass culture (Abrahamian, 1993). The new state-run organization, called the Basij (mobilization), was unlike the Shah's Rastakhiz with a top–down artificial structure which was poor in ideology and incapable of emerging as a real pro-establishment force if necessary. The Rastakhiz was the Shah's last attempt to consolidate his political bases by mobilizing the youth, whereas the Basij was the top priority for the new regime.

Emerging institutions

The Basij has so far been a factory to turn ordinary young people into ideological pro-regime forces able to defend the leaders and their principals. It was established in 1979 by the direct order of Khomeini under the name of "20-million army" in order to engage the youth, especially from lower-income layers, in the regime activities (Abdolmohammadi and Cama, 2020). Nevertheless, it gradually evolved and turned into a pillar of the country's security establishment (Ostovar, 2013, p. 345).

The Iranian youth are among the most politically active in Muslim countries, although the status of the youth in the post-revolutionary Iran has been mostly influenced by the political and military crises after the revolution (Memarian and Nesvaderani, 2010). Notably, the majority of warriors in the Iran–Iraq eight-year war (1980–1988) were young, with many of them even being teenage, and the Basij was specially expanded in this period. This brought hundreds of thousands of youths to recruitment centres (Ostovar, 2016, p. 86). In the 1980s, the Basij collaborated with the Revolutionary Committees, as the enforcers of new Islamic regulations and protectors of the revolution, to ensure internal security by identifying and eliminating the opponents who were later labelled as the enemy. Having severed the intelligence unit of the Islamic Revolutionary Guard Corps (IRGC), the Basij was ultimately incorporated into these corps. Thereafter, it came to light as an extensive network operating inspection patrols, intelligence-gathering, and security missions. It established a multitude of battalions in order to suppress social riots (Golkar, 2015, p. 109–110).

The regime later expanded the power of these young paramilitary forces again, an approach which was strengthened by the baby boomers in the 1980s. After Khomeini, Khamenei continued the policy of expanding the Basij and extending its scope of action. The Basij could be regular, active, special, and cadre of both the Basij and IRGC (Alfoneh, 2010). *Khatam-al-Anbia* (the title of Prophet Mohammad), the largest economic unit of the IRGC, owns at least 812 businesses and was involved in 1,500 construction projects from 1990 to 2007; the international sanctions have further encouraged the engagement of the IRGC in many industrial sections (Bazoobandi, 2015, p. 32). What is more, all state institutions, including universities and schools, are obliged to provide the Basij with an office and specific privileges. Aside from the Basij, the regime uses another organization whose members are mostly chosen from the youth: *Ansar-e Hezbollah* (the helpers of God's party), a partisan group which was founded in the 1990s and swiftly developed. Having a less structured and non-formal organization, it violently uses force against any social movement, even though it is not part of the official law enforcement (Memarian and Nesvaderani, 2010).

Such organizations lacked an apparent peacetime role; therefore, the leaders provided them with new areas of activity and the members were allocated domestic responsibilities, considering the value of their ideologically committed vast human resources (Ostovar, 2016, p. 142). These include many new duties, especially in internal security, post-war politics, law enforcement, special religious or political events, and moral policing, all of which take place under the name of cultural activism (Alfoneh, 2010). Although the open-source material does not reveal the exact number and the percentage of the paid, reserve, and volunteer forces, it is estimated to have around 11 million members. According to the British Home Office (2019), "the number of full-time, uniformed, and active members is at 90,000, with another 300,000 reservists and some 1 million that could be mobilised when necessary, … most of whom are believed to be between high school age and the mid-30s."

Basij members are provided with a large number of incentives such as gaining exemption from the mandatory military service, opportunities to secure financial loans, subsidized government housing, having access to subsidized food and household items, travel opportunities, free political and religious classes, admission quotas in university entrance examinations and preferred employment in government offices. Nevertheless, gaining access to an influential social network, where they can become part of an influential large institution which is backed directly by the Office of the Leader, should not be neglected (Ostovar, 2013, pp. 353–355). Having such an organized force under their rule, the establishment of Iran is capable of controlling and engineering civil activism. Over the last four decades, whilst the regime has acted as the machinery of limiting and containing civil society, the Basij, *Ansar-e Hezbollah*, and jihadi groups have massively grown as loyal forces. These forces were provided with another chance in the name of the battle with COVID-19.

COVID-19 outbreak: an ideological and political crisis

The history of the Islamic Republic has shown that every crisis may result in empowerment of the loyalist youth, and the COVID-19 outbreak was no exception. Indeed, it became a window of opportunity which led to a resurgence of the state-backed institutions such as the Basij in society. The virus, which emerged in a Wuhan city, China, open air wet market, was originally reported in late December 2019. It quickly transmitted from animals to humans and spread around the globe (Readfearn, 2020). The first COVID-19 death in Iran was officially reported on February 19, 2020 from Qom, a holy city hosting the Shrine of Fatima Masumeh, numerous seminaries, and religious centres (Hamshahri, 2020). The ideological importance of the city, which bears the title of "religious capital of Iran," made the Supreme Leader concerned about the potential damage to its religious credibility; therefore, it was reported that the authorities persisted with not accepting any infected case (BBC, 2020b).

The deaths linked to the coronavirus confirmed that approximately three to six weeks before the official announcement, the disease had existed in Qom and could easily spread due to the government's failure to follow safety protocols. The security forces of the Leader did not permit visitors to approach Khamenei at least a week before the announcement, a policy that lasted for almost nine months (Behravesh, 2020). At any rate, the virus spread in 24 out of 31 provinces of Iran in a period less than eight days from February 19. Confronting the epidemic, instead of closing religious and public places and quarantining Qom, the trustee of the Shrine called it a place for "healing spiritual and physical diseases" (Wright, 2020). The virus was officially asserted to be the enemy's pretext against the election. The politicization of the pandemic went even further when Khamenei accused the United States of creating the virus against Iran, adding that even if they sent medicines for the virus, that would be a means of making the virus persistent in Iran (Nasim, 2020).

The rise of the Basij and jihadi youths

On April 9, 2020, all public events had already been cancelled by the government; apparently, however, except for religious ones. Youth members of a state-backed jihadi group started so-called "happiness carnivals" in different districts of Tehran to celebrate the day with the idea that people would participate in this feast from their windows. In these caravans, religious youth walked alongside or rode in their cars next to a truck which carried huge amplifiers. In parallel, Khamenei opened the scene for military and quasi-military groups by speculating the crisis as a biological attack, which later paved the way for the military forces to operate a national biological manoeuvre. On the very next day after his speech, the Commander-in-Chief, General Bagheri, officially started the manoeuvre on streets of major cities and the Basij was the main force in this operation (BBC, 2020a).

At times of all kinds of crises, the Islamic Republic would certainly define a role for the Basij, *Ansar-e Hezbollah*, or jihadi youth to face the crisis and get involved in problem-solving processes under the command of the military. The presence of such groups in cities and rural areas became impressive in March when the virus outbreak rapidly increased throughout the country. Documentary reports about the activities of these groups were broadcasted repeatedly by national television and almost all state-sponsored news agencies reported on the operations. By way of illustration, the Basiji youths embarked on disinfecting public places in several cities before Nowruz, the Iranian new year, in March.

During the Nowruz holidays, the Basiji and jihadi groups employed their military tactics and methods in the public spheres and installed inspection stations or so-called health checkpoints at the entrance of almost all cities to impose some restrictions and prohibitions on inter-provincial traffic in order to control the outbreak, check the passengers' health conditions, and prevent non-resident people from entering their area. This resembles the activities of the members of the Revolutionary Committees at the outset of the 1979 revolution. The youth was again provided with the chance to emerge as a wing of the rulers. Furthermore, the Basiji youth and students of seminaries in some provinces distributed brochures with pieces of advice on hygiene in addition to organizing groups to disinfect public places. The Commander of Jihadi Operations Centre of the Basij announced that in addition to disinfecting public places, they are producing masks and disinfectants and distributing them in hospitals and amongst people. It was also claimed that the burial of coronavirus victims was being done by jihadi and Basij members as part of a national scheme entitled the Faithful Aid Exercise to protect the poor families and vulnerable groups from the virus (Mizan, 2020b).

Moreover, the Basij and the IRGC also embarked on so-called technical and scientific research on the virus and claimed that they were carrying out research on the vaccine and medicine development. Part of the Basij and *Ansar-e Hezbollah* figures officially prescribed several herbal medicines as the remedy for the health crisis under the name of Islamic medication, something that caused wide concerns. Besides, the Basij established and equipped field hospitals in many cities and dispatched military doctors and nurses to medical centres. IRGC commanders unveiled a device called *Mostaan-110*, claiming it as a magnetic COVID-19 detector capable of detecting the virus in five seconds from a radius of 100 metres. Nonetheless, it was soon criticized for being a failed inexpert effort (Middle East Eye, 2020).

It seems that the jihadi and Basiji youth in different bases and battalions attempted to overtake one another in presenting innovative projects. For instance, two jihadi groups in Khuzestan Province, ran the *Janbaz Yaar* (helper of the veteran) project to help disabled veterans with their daily shopping and other routines during the coronavirus outbreak (STnews, 2020). For instance, the Basij of Isfahan inspected 240 centres with a court order and detected hundreds of thousands of hoarded face masks and tons of sanitizer (IRNA, 2020). The plan involved 300,000 persons in teams whose mission was to go to random houses in order to screen the households and detect patients with coronavirus (IRNA, 2020). This expanded the Basij's scope of intervention in the public and private spheres. Nonetheless, part of the establishment named these activities as reminiscent of the youth presence on the frontlines of the eight-year war between Iran and Iraq four decades ago (Defa Press, 2020). For instance, a representative of the parliament stated that Basij forces have proved that they are the real children of the Islamic Revolution (Mizan, 2020a). Basij and the IRGC members were also assigned with municipal services such as picking up addicted people who had contracted the virus(Independent Persian, 2020). The Commander-General of the Police also announced that 320 people were arrested because of their online reports about the pandemic (Tabnak, 2020). Prior to that, at least two organizations had warned that print media were ordered to cease publication and many journalists were pressured and summoned because of publishing independent reports about the pandemic (IFJ, 2020; CPJ, 2020).

Conclusion

The emergence of a real vast loyal group of the youth came about only after the 1979 revolution, with all the similar attempts in the previous regime having failed. Four decades of recruiting, organizing, and marching loyal social movements on the streets are perfect examples of how the Iranian rulers have endeavoured to save the regime against internal and external pressures. In the recent case of the COVID-19 outbreak though, the leaders used several strategies with regards to the youth involvement through the Basij. The health crisis in 2020 became the season of the further growing state-sponsored organizations. Basij forces, as the regime's machinery, succeeded in expanding their areas of activity, fields of operations, and thus stabilizing their institutional dominance over the public and private spheres. However, the engagement of militia is never permanent and is rather short-term and mostly happens when there is a lack of collective action in society. Indeed, it is a battle against society under the name of helping people and a way to consolidate the militia's status and dominate the political sphere. Such activities are useful only when there is no widespread riot in the country and when society might accompany such groups out of fear, otherwise in times of social riots the militia itself can be a potential target for the dissidents.

References

Abrahamian, E. (1968). The Crowd in Iranian Politics 1905–1953. *Past & Present*, *41*(1), 184–210.

Abrahamian, E. (1969). The Crowd in the Persian Revolution. *Iranian Studies*, *4*(2), 128–150.

Abrahamian, E. (1993). *Khomeinism: Essays on the Islamic Republic*. London: University of California Press.

Abrahamian, E. (2008). *A History of Modern Iran*. New York: Cambridge University Press.

Alfoneh, A. (2010). The Basij Resistance Force. In R. Wright, *The Iran Primer: Power, Politics, and U.S. Policy* (pp. 59–65). Washington: United States Institute of Peace.

Bayandor, D. (2019). *The Shah, the Islamic Revolution and the United States*. Nyon: Palgrave Macmillan.

Bazoobandi, S. (2015). Iran's Economy and Energy: Back in Business? In P. Magri, and A. Perteghella, *Iran After the Deal: A Road Ahead* (pp. 24–47). Milan: Edizioni Epoké.

BBC (2020a, March 12). *Referring to the possibility of a "Biological Attack", Khamenei Ordered the Iranian Armed Forces to Establish a Corona Base.* Retrieved from BBC Persian: https://www.bbc.com/persian/iran-51855738.

BBC (2020b, August 3). *Corona Statistics Leak Reveals Iran's One-month Secrecy, Security Pressures Were the Reason for the Delay.* Retrieved from BBC Persian: https://www.bbc.com/persian/iran-features-53260478.

Behravesh, M. (2020, March 24). *The Untold Story of How Iran Botched the Coronavirus Pandemic.* Retrieved July 2020, from Foreign policy: https://foreignpolicy.com/2020/03/24/how-iran-botched-coronavirus-pandemic -response/.

Clarke, G. (1998). Non-Governmental Organizations (NGOs) and Politics in the Developing Countries. *Political Studies*, 46(1), 36–52.

Committee to Protect Journalists, CPJ (2020, March 20). *Amid Coronavirus Pandemic, Iran Covers Up Crucial Information and Threatens Journalists.* Retrieved from CPJ: https://cpj.org/2020/03/amid-coronavirus-pandemic-iran -covers-up-crucial-i/.

Defapress (2020, April 18). *Today's Youth Activities Against Corona Are Reminiscent of the Golden Years of Sacred Defence.* Retrieved from Defa Press: https://dnws .ir/392455.

Delli Carpini, M. X. (2000). Gen.Com: Youth, Civic Engagement, and the New Information Environment. *Political Communication*, 17(4), 341–349.

Earl, J., Maher, V. T., and Elliot, T. (2017). Youth, Activism, and Social Movements. *Sociology Compass*, 11(4), 1–14.

Erdmann, G. and Engel, U. (2006) *Neopatrimonialism Revisited: Beyond a Catch-all Concept.* GIGA Working Paper No. 16. Available at SSRN: https://ssrn.com /abstract=909183.

Firouzbakhch, H. (1988). A Structural-Demographic Approach to Revolution: The Case of the Revolution of 1979. *Civilisations*, 38(2), 85–104.

Foran, J. (1993). *Fragile Resistance: Social Transformation in Iran From 1500 To the Revolution.* Boulder: Westview Press.

Fowler, A. (1993). Non-governmental Organizations as Agents of Democratization: An African Perspective. *Journal of International Development*, 5(3), 325–339.

Ganji, M. (2002). *Defying the Iranian Revolution: From a Minister to the Shah to a Leader of Resistance.* Westport: Praeger.

Ghaffary, G. R. and Azizimehr, K. (2015). Government, Civil Society and Welfare Policies in Modern Iran. *Journal of Social Science for Policy Implications*, 3(2), 63–82.

Golkar, S. (2015). *Captive Society: The Basij Militia and Social Control in Iran.* New York: Columbia University Press.

Grant, W. (1989). *Pressure Groups, Politics and Democracy in Britain.* Hemel Hampstead: Philip Allan.

Halliday, F. (1979). *Iran, Dictatorship and Development.* New York: Penguin.

Hamshahri (2020, February 25). *When Was the First Case of Coronavirus Identified in Iran?* Retrieved from Hamshahri Online: http://hamshahrionline .ir/x68JQ.

Heydemann, S. (2007, October). *Upgrading Authoritarianism in the Arab World.* Saban Centre for Middle East Policy, Washington, DC: Brookings Institution, 13.

Home Office (2019, November). *Country Policy and Information Note Iran: Actors of protection.* Retrieved July 2020, from Gov.UK: https://assets.publishing .service.gov.uk/government/uploads/system/uploads/attachment_data/file /846810/Iran_-_AofP_-_CPIN_-_v1.0_-_Nov_2019_-_EXT.pdf.

Independent Persian (2020, August 04). Retrieved from Independent Persian: https://www.independentpersian.com/node/76151/.

The International Federation of Journalists, IFJ (2020, April 01). *Iran: Government Orders Nationwide Ban on Print Publications.* Retrieved from IFJ: https:// www.ifj.org/media-centre/news/detail/category/press-releases/article/iran -government-orders-nationwide-ban-on-print-publications.html.

The Islamic Republic News Agency, IRNA (2020, March 1). *Minister of Health: The Basij Disease Mobilization is Carried Out From the House to House.* Retrieved from IRNA: https://www.irna.ir/news/83697500/.

Jahanbegloo, R. (2013). *Democracy in Iran.* London: Palgrave Macmillan.

Karl, T. L. (1995). The Hybrid Regimes of Central America. *Journal of Democracy*, 6(3), 72–86.

Kazemi, F. (1996). Civil Society and Iranian Politics. In A. R. Norton, *Civil Society in the Middle East* (pp. 119–152). Leiden: Brill.

Kingdon, J. (1984). *Agendas, Alternatives, and Public Policies.* Boston: Little, Brown & Co.

Kubba, L. (2000). Arabs and Democracy: The Awakening of Civil Society. *Journal of Democracy*, 11(3), 84–90.

Lemarchand, R. and Legg, K. (1972). Political Clientelism and Development: A Preliminary Analysis. *Comparative Politics*, *4*(2), 149–178.

Liverani, A. (2008). *Civil Society in Algeria: The Political Functions of Associational Life.* Oxon: Routledge.

Lucey, A. (2019). Iranian Ulama & the CIA: The Key Alliance Behind the 1953 Iranian Coup D'état. *History in the Making*, *12*(1), 111–160.

Marx, K. (1954). *The Eighteenth Brumaire of Louis Bonaparte.* Moscow: Progress Publishers.

Memarian, O. and Nesvaderani, T. (2010). The Youth. In R. B. Wright, *The Iran Primer: Power, Politics, and U.S. Policy* (pp. 49–52). Washington: United States Institute of Peace.

Middle East Eye. (2020, April 23). *Iranian Press Review: Coronavirus Inventions Revealed by IRGC and Army Deemed 'Sci-fi.'* Retrieved from Middle East Eye: https://www.middleeasteye.net/news/iranian-press-review-irgc-army-compete -show-devices-detect-zap-coronavirus.

Mizan (2020a, April 19). *The Youth of the Third Generation of the Revolution Worked to Control the Corona Jihadi.* Retrieved from Mizan Online: https:// www.mizanonline.com/fa/news/613850/.

Mizan (2020b, April 20). *The Second Phase of the Jihadist Corona Services is Being Carried Out in the Form of a Faithful Relief Exercise.* Retrieved from Mizan Online: https://www.mizanonline.com/fa/news/614110/.

Muno, M. (2010, August 23). Conceptualizing and Measuring Clientelism. Paper to be presented at the workshop "Neopatrimonialism in Various World Regions." Hamburg: German Institute of Global and Area Studies.

Nasim (2020, March 22). *The United States is Accused of Producing Corona-Virus.* Retrieved from Nasim News Agency: https://www.nasimonline.ir/Content/Detail/2349552/.

Ostovar, A. (2013). Iran's Basij: Membership in a Militant Islamist Organization. *Middle East Journal, 67*(3), 345–361.

Ostovar, A. (2016). *Vanguard of the Imam: Religion, Politics, and Iran's Revolutionary Guards.* New York: Oxford University Press.

Ottaway, M. (2005). Civil Society. In P. Burnell, and V. Randall, *Politics in the Developing World* (pp. 166–185). Oxford: Oxford University Press.

Porta, D. D. and Diani, M. (1999). *Social Movements: An Introduction.* Victoria: Blackwell Publishing.

Poulson, S. C. (2006). *Social Movements in Twentieth-century Iran.* Lanham: Lexington Books.

Readfearn, G. (2020, April 28). *How Did Coronavirus Start and Where Did It Come From? Was It Really Wuhan's Animal Market?* Retrieved July 2020, from The Guardian: https://www.theguardian.com/world/2020/apr/28/how-did-the-coronavirus-start-where-did-it-come-from-how-did-it-spread-humans-was-it-really-bats-pangolins-wuhan-animal-market.

STnews (2020, July 12). *Dezfuli Youth Initiative to Help Veterans in the Days of Corona.* Retrieved September 2020, from STnews Website: http://stnews.ir/p=89134.

Tabnak (2020, May 9). *320 Persons Arrested for Rumours About Coronavirus.* Retrieved from Tabnak News Website: https://www.tabnak.ir/fa/news/977264/.

Wagner, H. L. (2010). *The Iranian Revolution.* New York: Chelsea House Publishers.

Wigell, M. (2008). Mapping 'Hybrid Regimes': Regime Types and Concepts in Comparative Politics. *Democratization, 15*(2), 230–250.

Wright, R. (2020, February 28). *How Iran Became A New Epienter of the Coronavirus Outbreak.* Retrieved July 2020, from Newyorker: https://www.newyorker.com/news/our-columnists/how-iran-became-a-new-epicenter-of-the-coronavirus-outbreak.

Yom, S. L. (2016). *From Resilience to Revolution: How Foreign Interventions Destabilize the Middle East.* New York: Columbia University Press.

4 Youth virtual activism in Morocco

The case fact-checkers

Mohammed Yachoulti and Hamza Bailla

Introduction

Activism can be defined as an action conducted by some active citizens to make other citizens aware that something is going wrong and involve them to seek remedies to get things in order. Activism is usually achieved by the citizens themselves, or with the help of the constitutional institutions such as the parliament, legislative assemblies, executive bodies, administration, and the judiciary. A democratic activist usually sets himself/herself as "a model of citizen virtues" (Young, 2001, p. 672). He/she is usually "committed to social justice and normative values" (ibid., pp. 672–673). He/she advocates the "idea that a politically responsible person ought to take positive action to promote these [values]" (ibid., p. 673). Activism "has played a major role in ending slavery, challenging dictatorships, protecting workers from exploitation, protecting the environment, promoting equality for women, opposing racism, and many other important issues" (Martin, 2007, p. 19). Yet, it has received relatively little attention from scholars (ibid.). Indeed, "most history is written about powerful and prominent people and about official systems and activities, such as governments, elections, militaries, and wars" (ibid., p. 25).

In this chapter, the purpose is not to review and discuss the theory of activism as it may appear, but the ultimate goal is to investigate fact-checking as an emerging journalistic brand and activism that has the potential to correct the inaccuracies in the public sphere and establish common ethical consensus/consent. Specifically, this study aims to explore and trace the profile and trajectory of Mustapha Fekkak, an online fact-checker, to understand his practices, and productions, and the impact he makes in the public sphere and his role in setting the stage for social movements to grow. The significance of this research resides in the fact that it tracks another form of activism that has emerged in parallel with developments in the Moroccan media landscape.

Youth activism in Morocco

Moroccan youth activism has its origins in the protectorate period and has since taken different shapes and forms and had different impacts. Moroccan youth activism started during the protectorate period when the first Moroccan students in France started to organize and agitate for an end to foreign rule in the last two decades of the French protectorate. They also criticized the authoritarian nature of French rule. After independence in 1956, Moroccan students founded the *Union Nationale des Etudiants du Maroc* (The National Union for Moroccan students) (UNEM) as an umbrella for student rights such as housing, scholarships, transportation subsidies, and employment opportunities after graduation. The new educational reform laws in the early 2000s allowed student representation in college and university presidential councils. The youth have been able to be politically involved through a variety of conventional forms of political participation. Indeed, they have the right to vote, to run for elections, and to adhere to or form a political party, an association, or a union (Zerhouni and Akesbi, 2016).

In 1991, unemployed MA and PhD holders, namely those who were active in UNEM, created the *Association Nationale des Diplômés Chômeurs du Maroc* (The National Association of Unemployed Graduates of Morocco) (ANDCM). Indeed "the emergence of the movement was fostered by several factors that converged at the end of the 1980s: a relatively liberal opening of political space, the notable reduction of the state's role as employer and the transformations of left-wing student unionism" (Badimon, 2018, p. 1). In 2011, the pro-democracy calls that swept the region inspired a number of young people to take action and initiate campaigns and struggles. The Moroccan youth launched the February 20 Movement which asked for freedom, equality, an end to corruption, better living conditions, education, labour rights, Amazigh rights, and many others. The struggle and activism led by this youth movement had immediate gains as Zerhouni and Akesbi (2016) summarized:

> Following the 2011 constitution, more spaces were created by the regime to provide ordinary citizens with channels to voice their opinions or to influence legislation and policies. These spaces are not youth-specific, but young people could benefit from them. The new constitution allowed the creation of the Consultative Council of Youth and Community Work (Art. 33), and introduced the principle of consultation with civil society organizations in designing, implementing and evaluating public policies (Art. 12). Other constitutional provisions provide the means for citizens to influence legislation through

the formulation of draft legislation or the presentation of petitions (Arts. 13 to 15). Following the 2011 legislative elections, the House of Representatives reserved 30 seats on the national list for young people.

(p. 4)

In sum, tracing Moroccan youth activism since the colonial period shows that they have always participated in the public sphere and political life through a variety of formal and informal channels. The subsequent section will track the development of fact-checking and its origins in Morocco.

Fact-checking trend

Fact-checking may be defined as "the assignment of a truth value to a claim made in a particular context" (Mihaylova et al., 2018). This new trend of fact-checking news and political claims is becoming prevalent all over the world. It is becoming a movement, which challenges not only the political elite but also journalism itself. It started as a temporary activity during US electoral campaigns and moved to be a permanent part in American media coverage by the Washington Post, FactCheck.org, and Politifact. This new media product has made these organizations more visible and recognized by major journalism awards (Graves et al., 2016).

Given the fact that the fact-checking trend was born during the 2007 US elections, it is safe to conclude that it is meant to protect democracy from the oversupply of misinformation of the competing parties during the heated electoral campaigns. This tradition has its roots in the process of selecting claims and statements for fact-checking. FactCheck.org states clearly on its methodology page: "Our topics vary slightly depending on the election cycle". As for the process of research, there is no agreed procedure for fact-checkers to follow. However, Politifact has developed seven steps to verify the veracity of content after selecting it: "1) Ask the person making the claim for evidence. 2) Look for what other fact-checkers have found before you. 3) Do a Google search? 4) Search the Deep Web. 5) Look for experts with different perspectives. 6) Check out some books. 7) Anything else? [to take some time to ask if something is missing]" (Angie, 2014).

Fact-checking is subject to the gatekeeping effect like other types of journalism. Also, as maintained by Uscinski and Butler, the main problem of the contemporary fact-checkers is the binary opposition between a fact and a lie, and the difficulty or even the impossibility to verify certain political claims. This is due to many reasons. First, using the terminology of true, false, mostly true, or other expressions to assess political claims is not accurate. Second, fact-checkers often check political claims about policies and their future impact, which are subject to different variables that need more scientific research. Third, the strategy to divide political statements into fragments and rate them is ambiguous because giving an overall rating of "mostly true" gives the audience the impression that all the claims are true (Uscinski and Butler, 2013).

Fact-checking in Morocco

Unlike the global trend of fact-checkers which was driven by professional values to restore trust in journalism, fact-checkers in Morocco are citizen journalists who are not affiliated to any media corporations. They are a limited number of Moroccan youths who produce organized informative content for the public to offer background information about a large variety of issues in a fact-checking style. Put differently, fact-checking in Morocco has originated in a different context and has been pioneered by a group of young citizens whose focus is forming free and independent online communities. They aim to provide background information and verify claims and information in the Moroccan media landscape. They are limited in number and are not affiliated to any media corporations.

Based on the fieldwork of this study, only four YouTubers and activists can be classified as fact-checkers in Morocco; they have an easily distinguished style of separating facts and opinions, providing background factual information, and are transparent about their sources. These four are Najib Mokhtari, Othmane Safsafi, Mustapha Fekkak, and Marwan Alaouie Mharzi. Najib Mokhtari is a Moroccan engineer who makes videos of popular science and critical thinking in Moroccan society. His videos are aimed at a broad public; they explain issues using scientific methods. Othamane Safsafi is a Moroccan PhD student who makes videos about popular science and critical thinking. His videos are known for criticizing what is called "scientific miracles in the Quran."

Mustapha Fekkak, known as Mustapha Swinga, is a famous YouTuber in Morocco. He is also an artist, producer, and manager of the Accoustic Company. He is famous for his YouTube channel *Aji Tafham* (Let's understand) which explains topics related to social problems, sensitive political issues, and the economy. In his videos, he uses a mix of investigation and humour to explain and illustrate his message. He has reached nearly half a million subscribers on his YouTube channel, and many of his videos exceed a million views.

Marwane is a state engineer and founder of carte.ma, an on-demand service that manages photographs of the streets of Morocco. Marwane Alaouie Mharzi is also an influential YouTuber in Morocco specializing in explaining factual historical events in Morocco. This chapter, however, focuses on Mustapha Swinga and his *Aji Tafham* YouTube channel. This is due to the following reasons. First, unlike Mokhtari whose videos focus on and explain issues using scientific methods, Safsafi whose videos are known for criticizing what is called "scientific miracles in the Quran," and Mharzi who has various field interests, Mustapha Fekkak or Swinga produces videos explaining topics related to sensitive social, economic, and political issues. The issues and topics tackled in his videos have stirred reactions from all factions of Moroccan society and resulted in long public debates. Second, Swinga's videos are addressed to all Moroccans regardless of their educational and social backgrounds and are meant to fill a gap in the Moroccan media landscape and produce a neutral narrative on sensitive political and economic issues. The videos produced by the other fact-checkers, however, target only a category of Moroccans who are interested in the kind of topics they tackle, a fact which explains the difference in their number of subscribers. Mustapha Swinga has 633,000 subscribers, Najib Mokhtari, 206,000, Othmane Safsafi, 106,000, and Marwane Alaouie Mharzi 410,000. Also, Swinga's videos have had millions of views, whereas other fact-checkers have neither the same consistency of production, nor the same potential impact in the public sphere.

Methodology

The main aim of this chapter is to consider fact-checking as an emerging journalistic brand and activism that has the potential to correct inaccuracies in the public sphere and establish common ethical consensus/consent. To this effect, the chapter uses the cases of Mustapha Fekkak, known as Swinga, to understand this emerging phenomenon in Morocco. The chapter focuses mainly on the operation system of this activist, his strategies of content generation, and the impact he makes in the public sphere. As the fact-checking content on YouTube in Morocco is still rare or marginalized, the data is collected through personal interviews with Swinga and other two fact-checkers (Najib Mokhtari, Othmane Safsafi) following him through his channel *Aji Tafham* (Let's understand) and posts on Facebook, Instagram, and YouTube. The chapter has also made use of two journalistic interviews with Mustapha Fakkak. The first interview was broadcasted on MedRadio channel on December 21, 2018, through its weekly episode *"Fi Kafass Itiham"* (In the dock) which invites influential Moroccan figures in politics, media, art, and sport. The second journalistic interview was broadcasted on Chada TV on May 18, 2020, on its weekly episode of *The Ktotbi Tonight*. The episode invites two or three stars, who could be artists, comedians, writers, singers, media figures, or athletes to introduce their topics and bring to life the memory of their professional achievements. Both journalistic interviews were very helpful to get more data on his content and activism. All the interviews were transcribed, translated to English, and then coded using ATLAS.ti software. This has provided the possibility to create codes, classify them into themes, and move across interviews and codes more efficiently to compare responses

Results

The process of coding and analysing the interviews has resulted in six themes, detailed as follows:

Swinga's production motivations

Motivation is a key element in understanding the reasons for Swinga's existence. This YouTuber has both shared and personal interest in the content he produces. His aim is to share content-based facts about sensitive issues in a very objective style to fill the gap in the Moroccan media landscape. Common interest is his strongest driver to produce content and videos, Swinga says:

> Frankly, the choice of my topics depends on the public choice, and my wish comes at the second rank. The first reason is the general vision that people have to understand, depending on what I have understood …

In fact, this idea is expressed in his channel *Aji Tafham*, which includes a variety of videos on different issues. This includes explaining economic concepts, legal procedures, taxation, social problems, new policies, etc. *Aji Tafham* also seeks to raise the awareness of political and socio-economic problems. Choosing a topic like the cost of fuel in Morocco, Swinga tried to give the audience tools through which to understand the news and political reforms. To explain more, Swinga says:

> My objective is to explain to the public the basics of existence, and with these bases one can ask questions. This is my objective from my work. I try to help viewers to ask the existential questions, like, what are your rights? What are your obligations?

Explaining the basics is providing background information to the public. This is an important technique to help them make sense of the news, ask the right questions, and involve them in the public debate.

Production process of Swinga's fact-checking

The personal motivation to share fact-checking videos without any involvement from other media organizations is having an impact on the creative process of making videos online. Also, branding his channel as investigation is setting the standards high. The accuracy of facts and the clarity of the message is a priority. As a result, the process of getting information is demanding and sometimes challenging, depending on the possible influence of each video on the public. Swinga's channel *Aji Tafham* covers subjects related to political, economic, and social issues. This is the reason why he defines it as a mixture of arts and investigation. To use his own words, he says that "the work I do is related to investigation, it's a mixture between research investigation and art." For example, to prepare a video about the problem of "teachers contracts," he started by checking official websites and government documents to get an idea about the official version of the problem, then he contacted the teachers to get information about their side of the problem. However, this process does not go with problems and difficulties. In this regard, he says:

> Sometimes I get difficulties in getting access to information … and sometimes I face closed doors, but other times, some people are helpful, especially those in the government. From a programmatic perspective, if they don't give me the precise information, I may get it wrong, and the video will have a different impact, so it's better that they give me accurate information to work properly. At the end if the information is correct, and the fact is dispatched, everyone will benefit.
>
> (Interview with MedRadio, 2018 in Kifach TV, 2018)

Getting access to reliable information about political, social, or complex economic problems can be a baffling job in Morocco. Still, Swinga points out that there is an openness to give him more information. He also insists that there is a growing understanding within many authority officials who think that these videos are important and beneficial to promote the official version of the story.

Swinga's interaction with the public

Social media has become an established form to become informed about different topics. Typically, Swinga believes that the social aspect has made it an alternative to mainstream media. It is not only a simple tool that helps content producers share their content, but it is also a space where they get feedback, learn from their audience, and from each other. Nevertheless, this relationship can have its ups and downs as well as challenges in an online toxic environment.

Social networks are about networking and keeping in touch with the audience. However, like any social interaction, online or offline, there are a number of informal rules fact-checkers should stick to. One of them is that a fact-checker cannot publish or post on the internet and then sign out. Therefore, after posting any content, Swinga pays close attention to the feedback of his followers and audience. It is not just having a quick look at the comments section, but in fact it is a long demanding process of learning from justified criticism, answering questions, and getting suggestions for other topics to cover. As for emotional comments or personal attacks, Swinga reports that he ignores them most of the time.

Discussion

Analysing Swinga's answers in the three interviews and observing the details about his productions make the researchers confident enough to claim that the best way to define his role in Moroccan society is a form of activism. He is a "fact" activist; he holds a strong belief in the importance of facts in any societal debate, and he defends investigation, fights misinformation in mainstream media and social media, and preserves neutrality in cases of ideological differences. This kind of activism is led without any journalistic institutional affiliation, unlike the global media market which is adopted by leading journalistic institutions (Graves et al., 2016).

Along with three other Moroccan fact-checkers, Swinga fills a gap within the Moroccan media landscape. Using Moroccan Arabic enlarges the audience of online content and improves the understanding of what was regarded as complex for the general public. Swinga's work is a movement against misinformation, and other types of ideologically biased ideas. It is also struggle for a fact-based debate. To clarify, the *Aji Tafham* channel tries to draw a big picture of several political, social, and economic complex problems. Swinga opts for neutrality as a safer strategy to present his content, by giving voice to all concerned parties. This may be explained by two reasons. First, it is safer because it helps him to maintain better relationships with all parties, which can be helpful to get access to information. Second, it helps avoid being accused of fact-checking what cannot be checked, like the criticism directed against professional fact-checkers in the world, as explained in the review of literature by Uscinski and Butler (2013). Judging information as accurate or not, false or true is not evident in topics like policymaking or social problems.

Another promising finding is that despite the fact that access to information is very challenging in Morocco, and there is a bureaucratic structure which creates a lot of restrictions, there are hints that media capital acquired in the social media can ease the way a little bit. Swinga has declared that he faces many problems and closed doors in the process of research. This chapter subscribes to John Thomson's definition which extended this concept to the "capacity to intervene in the course of events, to influence the actions of others and indeed to create events, by means of the production and transmission of symbolic forms" (Couldry, 2003). Thus, the more influence a fact-checker has, the easier it is to get information.

A similar pattern of results can be understood from the pressure exerted on Swinga, from his fans, or marginalized groups to discuss a topic. Swinga has received no financial benefits from the content he produces, which is similar to Bourdieu's description of small-scale production of content. He has less economic capital, but on the other hand, he is acquiring a growing symbolic and media capital that enables him to intervene in key moments of national debate. With perseverance and hard work, he has managed to effectively convert his media capital into economic capital; he has succeeded in setting up his company and getting indirect financial support and symbolic capital from his media presence online. Now, he is famous for his videos in the *Aji Tafham* YouTube channel, and his company offers content production services using his style of combining humour and investigation. Economic capital, like financial support, is important in pushing for more objectivity in the Moroccan public sphere. Nevertheless, Swinga avoids accepting money that may threaten his credibility, independence, and public trust.

Habermas (1991) believes that commercial forces dominate the public sphere in the contemporary media landscape, and big media corporations are setting the agenda for people depending on their interests. As a result, with the rise of social networks, Kellner (2014) seized the opportunity to expand Habermas' public sphere with the new global technologies, where anyone can express his views, discuss issues of public interest, and participate in social changes. However, he failed to theorize more about the structure surrounding this new environment. Bourdieu (1996), instead of blaming the growing impact of the economic power in the degradation of the public sphere, puts the economic field as part of the game. Swinga has expressed how getting more funding is going to sustain his work and improve the quality of videos.

The fact-checking trend is evolving in Morocco. Swinga recently started shooting videos instead of crafting sophisticated animations to explain his message, to reduce the cost and to release videos in moments of heated debate. If he uploads a video after the public discussion has faded, which is often a few days, it will get limited exposure. The results cast a new light on the importance of symbolic capital in making an impact on the public sphere (Kellner, 2014). Habermas (1991) believes in the power of arguments as powerful tools. However, reaching out to people with more symbolic power is an essential step in fighting for any cause or working for social change. Taking into account the situation of journalism in Morocco, and how it is highly politicized, many social movements find their way to get through to the public agenda by gaining the support of fact-checkers like Swinga.

It is hardly accurate to claim that citizen journalists are either promoting hegemonic propaganda or alternative discourse, as described by El-Issawi (2016). Swinga goes beyond the traditional classification of citizen journalism. Fact-checkers, as a new trend online, which is demonstrating the diversity of the online content, are siding with facts. Fact-checkers can play the role of an "intermediary layer" as described by Sienkiewicz (2014). In a moment of uncertainty and social unrest, factual content is crucial to help people make sense of the news. The online public sphere in Morocco can be understood from Swinga's perspective as a site for a tense struggle between different fields as described by Pierre Bourdieu in his book *The Rules of Art: Genesis and Structure of the Literary Field* (1996). In a nutshell, it seems like the Habermas public sphere is revived in these online communities, with the potential effect of discussions based on facts, and everyone can express himself/herself.

Conclusion

What distinguished this study is its endeavour to shed light on a new activism in Morocco. Swinga is setting the example in explaining complex social, economic, and political issues to online users. His aim is to reveal facts, create a virtual public sphere, and act as an inspirational source for actors and movements calling for positive change. Also, his commitment to a more interactive approach to communication and his ability to accept others' points of view reflect a kind of respect for the public, a contribution to online debates, and move towards more transparency and engagement in redressing and correcting the chaotic situation in social and mainstream media.

References

Angie, H. (2014). 7 Steps to better fact-checking. *PolitiFact*. Retrieved from https://www.politifact.com/article/2014/aug/20/7-steps-better-fact-checking/.

Badimon, E. M. (2018): From contestation to conciliation: social networks and engagement in the unemployed graduates movement in Morocco, *Social Movement Studies*. 113–129. DOI: 10.1080/14742837.2018.1540347.

Bourdieu, P. (1996). *The Rules of Art: Genesis and Structure of the Literary Field*. Translated by Susan Emanuel. Stanford, CA: Stanford University Press. https://doi.org/10.4324/9780203131527.

Chada (May 18, 2020). *The Kotbi Tonight: Mustafa Swinga & Amine Raghib*. Available at YouTube. https://www.youtube.com/watch?v=dw0jeipu2Ss.

Couldry, N. (2003). Media meta-capital: Extending the range of Bourdieu. *Theory and Society*, *32*(5–6), 653–677. https://doi.org/10.1023/B:RYSO.0000004915.37826.5d.

El Issawi, F. (2016). *Moroccan National Media: Between Change and Status Quo.* LSE Middle East Centre Report. London: London School of Economics and Political Science, Middle East Centre.

Graves, L., Nyhan, B., and Reifler, J. (2016). Understanding Innovations in Journalistic Practice: A Field Experiment Examining Motivations for Fact-Checking. *Journal of Communication*, *66*(1), 102–138. https://doi.org/10.1111/jcom.12198.

Habermas, J. (1991). *Theory and Practice*. Translated by John Viertel. Oxford, United Kingdom: Cambridge Beacon Press.

Kellner, D. (2014). Habermas, the public sphere, and democracy. In D. Boros and J. M. Glass (Eds), *Re-Imagining Public Space: The Frankfurt School in the 21st Century* (19–43). New York, NY. Palgrave Macmillan. https://doi.org/10.1057/9781137373311_2.

Martin, B. (2007). Activism, social and political. Published by Gary L. Anderson and Kathryn G. Herr (Eds), *Encyclopedia of Activism and Social Justice* (pp. 19–27). Thousand Oaks, CA: Sage. Retrieved from http://www.bmartin.cc/pubs/07Anderson.html.

Mihaylova, T., Nakov, P., Marquez, L., Barron-Cedeno, A., Mohtarami, M., Karadzhov, G., and Glass, J. (2018). *Fact Checking in Community Forums.* Cornell University, 18–22. http://arxiv.org/abs/1803.03178.

Sienkiewicz, M. (2014). Start making sense: a three-tier approach to citizen journalism. *Media, Culture & Society*, *36*(5). https://doi.org/10.1177/0163443714527567.

Uscinski, J. E. and Butler, R. W. (2013). The epistemology of fact checking. *Critical Review*, *25*(2), 162–180. https://doi.org/10.1080/08913811.2013.843872.

Young, I. M. (2001). Activist challenges to deliberative democracy. *Political Theory*, *29*(5), 670–690.

Zerhouni, S. and Akesbi, A. (2016). *Youth Activism in Morocco: Exclusion, Agency and the Search for Inclusion*, Working Paper No. 15. https://www.iai.it/sites/default/files/p2y_15.pdf.

5 Challenges to youth civic engagement and community development in Syria

Alaa Hadid

Introduction

Young people comprise the majority of most Arab countries today and were the engine for change during the past decade that witnessed what was called the "Arab Spring" (United Nations, 2020). The most educated of young people who led the waves of change in many Arab countries with the aim of consolidating their respective nations' contribution in the political arena and putting an end to all aspects of oppression practised on them for years. The Arab spring brought up more interaction between civil society and state institutions. This interaction aimed at raising the voices of marginalized citizens and most importantly, youth (Fioramonti and Heinrich, 2007). There is no doubt that now youth are perceived differently and more seriously after mobilizing for such huge changes. Regardless of the results, it is evident that the youth demonstrated an unprecedented ability to become an integral part of the social transformations of the Arab Spring in 2011. The UN (2020) defines young people (female and male) as those who are above 15 and under 24 years of age. This age group comprises 16% of the global population (1.2 billion people). This number will grow in the coming decade until 2030 to be nearly 1.3 billion (UN, 2020).

Young people's civic engagement takes different forms, like being part of social organizations, volunteering, being part of social change or awareness-raising initiatives, etc. Civic engagement is even broader than political engagement because it involves all aspects related to society while political engagement is related only to the political sphere (Ekman and Amnå, 2012). Levine (2007) and Battistoni (2013) use different terms of engagement with society as social capital, public agency, community building, public work, social engagement, and civic or public leadership. Kaldor (2003), however, defines civil society as a process of engagement "the process through which individuals negotiate, argue, and struggle against or agree with each other and with the centres of political and economic authority." Community members' engagement in civil society activism aims, in many instances, at managing conflict and in better cases aims at preventing conflict. Paffenholz (2009) defines civil society actors who engage in non-governmental organizations (NGOs), unions, faith-based organizations, associations, and all other similar non-governmental associations. Local peacebuilding lies at the heart of civil society initiatives. Peacebuilding activities, which take place before, during, and after conflicts, aim at promoting peacebuilding (Galtung and Fischer, 2013).

To understand young people's civic engagement and peacebuilding from a Syrian perspective, the author interviewed a number of youths who engage to promote community development in Syria despite the security constraints and the political polarization. The author interviewed young people who are primarily engaged in local civil society activities in the Syrian context.

The Syrian context

Prior to 2011, civil society in Syria barely existed and the level of oppression practised by the authorities meant this domain was dominated exclusively by government actors. Local NGOs, as well as any initiative group, could only function after obtaining approval from the state authorities. The process of approval is a highly bureaucratic and lengthy process. The "Syrian Trust for Development," headed and founded by Asma al-Assad, was one of many examples (Kawakibi, 2012). Syrians inspired by the Arab spring mobilized to protest against the regime and called for political and social freedom. The protest turned into violent confrontations and drove the country to an endless civil war which continues today. The regime controlled food and healthcare supplies to the protesting areas and districts which made it impossible for international aid organizations to operate on the ground in areas outside the government's control. Civil society organizations (CSOs) multiplied in number and started to serve the wider public, owing to a changing environment and the internal displacement of thousands of people (Crawford, 2015).

These CSOs, however, needed government approval and supervision in order to function, which made them obliged to register with government institutions. This led to the reformation or "taming" of civil society initiatives to perform the role of local government but still be considered as emergent from the local civil society (Khalaf, 2015). Other types of NGOs are those run by Syrian diaspora living outside the country. These are known as diaspora organizations. Syrian civil society is "slowly consolidating itself into more stable entities, strengthening its ability to respond to the humanitarian crisis" (Serwer, 2014). Given the difficulties faced by international

NGOs in providing support to the local communities, they must partner with government institutions to deliver aid. International actors should also collaborate with local actors to fill the gap (Aykut, 2018). These circumstances have already imposed barriers to effective engagement by young people and their contribution to their communities during the civil war.

Youth's challenges

The dramatic events of the Arab spring have proven that youth can be catalysts of change in their respective communities. Arab youth, as well as all other society members have experienced injustices for decades which provoked them to group and revolt as a result. This provoked the Arab communities to see youth in a different light; to see them as assets for change, not only as recipients. The youth are suffocated by the prevailing economic systems that cripple them from making the changes they aspire to. Unemployment proves to be a recurring issue in the Arab world and especially among the youth. Youth unemployment has reached up to 27.17% of the population in the Arab world. This percentage is especially high in Syria where it reached 20.94% of the overall population in 2019. Challenges facing young people in the field of community development and peacebuilding are many, including practitioners and to a lesser extent policymakers, and are the ones who are hit directly by these challenges. According to the United Nations Development Programme (UNDP), the poverty line increased in the Arab world by about 37% compared to before 2010.

Young people who work in NGOs or who start their own initiatives are the ones who lack resources to achieve high goals that can compete with the goals of international NGOs (INGOs) because of many reasons. Some of these reasons are the lack of experiences, lack of time (as many are either university students or have a full-time job), lack of funds, etc. Youth CSOs need to support the diversity of the groups they represent and the diverse goals they pursue as Paffenholz and Spurk (2006) discussed. The importance of engaging young people considers "composition and characteristics of civil society in specific country context and specific functions of civil society" (Paffenholz and Spurk, 2006). Youth CSOs are mostly overwhelmed by the number of challenges they face when they come up with some initiatives. Syrian young people, however, have found migration as a solution. There are many incentives for youth to migrate and these are (and not limited to): improving their quality of life and well-being and receiving a higher income, attaining better professional and employment opportunities, receiving better education and degrees, among many other factors (Mulderig, 2013; Khouri et al., 2011). Gallup's (2010) regional survey

(Silatech Index) concluded that about 30% of Arab youth intend to migrate whenever they have the opportunity to do so.

With the evolving political context of the Arab region, new opportunities emerge and now it is high time for youth to lead this change. For example, one of the most rewarding opportunities that Tunisian youth reaped after the revolution is freedom of speech. UNESCO (2011) discussed youth civic engagement from the perspective of economic participation of young people in the Arab region. UNESCO (2011) also examined two major challenges facing youth in the Arab countries as participation in the economic sphere and youth engagement in the Arab regional context after the Arab spring. The youth, referred to as a "youth bulge," were one of the main catalysts for the Arab uprisings (UNESCO, 2011). However, Syrian youth are not yet free to practise freedom of speech because the revolution in Syria was transformed into a crisis with many inter-state and intra-state actors involved. Yet, we cannot deny the power of words spread through social media that initiated the call for change by young people.

Young people's case studies

Despite these difficult circumstances, young people have been powerful and agents for fundamental change. They recognize the potential they have and if they figured out how to deploy it in innovative ways. They can participate in creating their future by being engaged in civic society activities to be part of the decision-making process they have been alienated from for decades. Here, young people share their experiences and stories of civic engagement in Syria.

Waseem Al-Sakhleh

Waseem Al-Sakhleh, a Damascene born in 1993 and not even 30 years of age, has so far demonstrated leadership capacity that cannot be overlooked. He is currently a research assistant at the Syrian Initiative, a Joint Survey Society in Beirut, and has led a considerable number of youth initiatives in Syria aimed at peacebuilding and community development. A Master's student specializing in Islamic–Christian relations, a a BA holder in Political Science from Damascus University and a student at the Faculty of Mass Communication at Damascus University, Waseem tries in his initiatives to make a positive change in the Syrian community not only during the Syrian crisis, but even before its start. He started voluntary activities in his school and neighbourhood before going beyond that to be a member of civil society chambers in the Geneva Peace Negotiations of 2017.

Starting from the very beginning of the crisis in Syria, Waseem volunteered with a group of youths to provide shelters in Damascus for the internally displaced people (IDPs) making sure that IDPs are provided with food and healthcare. Waseem has been a member of the Board of Directors of the "Syrian Family Association" where he volunteered for ten years providing healthcare and psychological support for IDPs through mobile clinics. Support to these initiatives mostly came from community in-kind donations. Waseem highlighted during the interview that their initial response as a volunteering youth group "created gaps" which remained as weak points after the group would leave the neighbourhood or area they support. It is worth mentioning here that humanitarian response in conflict-affected areas, when it lacks support from governmental institutions or international organizations, can be less effective because of the lack of organized work in the recipient communities, which in turn can waste much of the effort expended in voluntary activities (Brown et al., 2014).

Looking at Waseem's experience, the researcher enquired about the extent to which the international organizations considered creating synergies with similar youth initiatives on the ground. Unfortunately, it is not the case in Syria. INGOs come with pre-designed agendas and are ready-made to apply them regardless of the context in which they operate. Incidents like the monthly distribution of items to beneficiaries that they used once and then would sell in the local market have created parallel markets that can only do more damage to the already shaky Syrian economy. Not recognizing the real needs of our beneficiaries leads to waste and duplication of efforts and Waseem, like the Syrian and Arab youth in general, has grassroots experiences that come from the communities we design our objectives in project proposals to ultimately support. If we fail to create links with them, we are failing to achieve our goals in localizing humanitarian action and empowering the communities we serve. This will lead to losing the trust of our beneficiaries and will only make us agents to cover immediate pressing needs with no consideration of the long-term effects of our response.

In line with achieving the humanitarian–development–peacebuilding nexus approach and moving from humanitarian aid delivery to long term development and later peacebuilding goals in societies that were once subject to conflicts, Waseem in one of his initiative groups decided to set aside aid delivery and move to deeper problems within Syrian society that had their roots before the 2011 crisis. The group tackled issues related to sexual education for youth at schools and it involved teachers as well as part of awareness raising of this issue. It is not to say that humanitarian aid response is ineffective, but it is the first step to move towards development and later achieve peace in conflict-affected areas.

On challenges, Waseem highlighted the difficulties of issuing a licence for initiatives to be registered as local organizations recognized by the government. Long bureaucratic processes that take months aborted the spontaneous volunteer groups' hopes of being part of the humanitarian aid scene in Syria. Added to that is the element of commitment embedded in registering groups. Many young people in Syria today look for ways of getting visas out and, as mentioned earlier, this creates considerable challenges for the civic community to develop. Acquired knowledge of managing hindrances the youth may face has been accumulated throughout the years of their response to the humanitarian crisis in Syria. These are newly acquired "tactics" that youth initiating humanitarian support programmes started to learn and deploy in order to make sure their initiatives are not stopped by the government. These tactics mainly revolve around engaging one of the recognized authority figures in neighbourhoods like the "mukhtar," who is the head of a village or a neighbourhood, to ensure government approval of the conducted initiatives and activities as Al-Sakhleh reported they would usually do.

Another tactic is conducting activities under the name of an already registered local organization to avoid the long bureaucratic process of registration. Youth groups can conduct their activities inside religious entities (mosques and churches) because such entities enjoy a wider margin of freedom. The 2011 crisis not only affected the humanitarian work in Syria, it "revolutionized it," as Waseem noted. At the beginning of the crisis, civil society was a means to support the needy voluntarily then the government hindered the work of local NGOs in affected areas as a way of containing the protesters. As time passed, the youth recognized that they would need to transform this voluntary work into a source of income generation, and it is here that the youth turned to employment opportunities in the INGOs and NGOs.

Waseem noted that humanitarian responses to youth initiatives mainly consisted the middle and lower classes in society and it was never the rich who took the lead in such initiatives. This brought such initiatives closer to the communities served and enabled the youth to receive more donations from ordinary people. Trust building is key in humanitarian response and can be a determining factor when it comes to international organizations' interventions, and it is beyond the scope of this chapter to provide a detailed analysis of such instances. But how can the Syrian youth be competitive in the "humanitarian response market" that emerged in Syria after 2011? Earlier stages of community development projects in Syria were of a much lower quality than the current INGOs' response and these projects were of very limited funds, limited access, and highly monitored by the government. After the events of 2011, massive displacement made local community members' engagement inevitable. This engagement did not come without its shortcomings, for there were limited sources to acquire the necessary knowledge to reach a professional level in this field. Civil society responders had to make mistakes and learn from these mistakes; some have learnt from peer mishaps. Others had the "luxury" of receiving quality training from an international institution. Another issue on funding is the inability of the local NGOs to keep up with the high pace and high level of professionalism INGOs can bring. This means that local NGOs had to follow the INGOs' agendas and implemented projects. This has become a mode followed for almost a decade now when it comes to humanitarian response. Waseem said:

> if an International organization decides to implement a psychological support project for beneficiaries in a given area, you'll see NGOs following this rhythm. We reach a state when everyone is doing psychological support projects and no guarantee for the prolongation of funds.

Waseem pointed out the issue of polarization in different regions and how this issue is affecting the deliverables of NGOs and INGOs. Individuals belonging to a given community, sect, or group are ignored when it comes to the training and benefits that are attained from different communities, sects, or groups. If you are working in the areas subject to government rule, you are technically affiliated with them and the opposite is true with regard to the opposition areas. Areas that are subject to government rule are much more supported than other areas, of course. A huge gap is created between civil society workers inside Syria and those who are outside. This gap is widened by time and neither the government nor the national and international actors are making efforts to bridge it. With the international sanctions applied on the country, it is nearly impossible for Syrians to get visas to travel abroad and receive proper training or study. In comparison, Syrians living outside Syria (with the exception of neighbouring countries hosting refugees such as Turkey, Jordan, Syria, and Lebanon) are receiving quality training and quality education. This gap is getting bigger in time and is separating civil society actors inside the country from those who are outside. This issue is referred to by several interviewees and is a concern for many on the ground. Waseem also highlighted the benefits of being part of peacebuilding initiatives in Syria. "Building on almost a decade of work in this field, youth in our civil society gained an insurmountable experience and were able to build a network of connections that can serve them".

Ali Nassr Abdullah

A cardiologist who has been involved in humanitarian work in Syria for eleven years now. A winner of the prize of the "Ten Most Distinguished Youth" award for the year 2020 at the national level in the category of leadership in humanitarian action and the founder and chairman of a local NGO named "Salam" which translates as "peace". Oxfam and UNDP were two of the many INGOs Ali had work experiences with. Ali initiated a youth project licensed as part of the Salam Organization projects licensed by the Ministry of Social Affairs and Labour in Syria. The project is called "Youngo" and aims at investing community capital, uniting energies, and cooperation, to establish initiatives aimed at enhancing community cohesion and strengthening relationships between members of society. In this 18-month-old project, special focus is made to utilize the experiences of the Syrian youth that aim at contributing to the rebuilding of their communities. The objectives of the project revolve around three basic aspects of development – service – public – concern. The project aims at involving community groups to help each other by enhancing the sense of responsibility among community members to help the most affected families (financial – food – health). The second aspect is developmental, where the project aims at building a bridge of relationships, partnership, and cooperation between various sectors, companies, and capital with non-profit and international organizations. On the public affairs side, the project focuses on the most important issues that every Syrian youth should care about.

On how they manage to cover the shortage in expertise in their project, Ali reported having all members of the committee responsible for their projects, headed by him, as being former or current INGO staff. They work on transferring the expertise they gained from working with professionals in international organizations to support their own. At the same time, INGOs should beware of the importance of connecting with activists on the ground. They are locals and are more capable of assessing the field and the needs. Ali advised young activists who aim at starting peacebuilding initiatives to be patient and make sure they develop their skills as time passes.

Maher Alabdullah

Maher Alabdullah is a social humanitarian worker, combining music, passion, and compassion to deliver social services to youth, children, and elderly people. He believes that everyone deserves happiness in life. Therefore, he plays an essential role in the community to deliver a good time through music. Maher's voluntary work is not limited to SARC and JCI but extended to other organizations in the Aleppo community. Maher is currently working as a logistics officer with Oxfam with many previous experiences in the non-profit sector. Above all, he plays guitar, and he has been a teacher for more than 11 years. Maher believes that music extends peace, and he is using his talent to this end. As a volunteer with SARC, he conducts weekly "music sessions" with people in Aleppo who live at an elderly home. "First couple of visits," Maher reports, "were short intro-ductory visits to the elderly home and we had little interaction with those people. Soon, the situation changed hugely. When we go to meet them now, we are given dessert and many other things". Maher reported the huge diffi-culties they had to face as they were engaged in peacebuilding initiatives at the early stages of the Syrian war. "I had to continue playing the guitar when I heard shelling outside". The same successful experience was reported by Maher in another elderly home called "Basmet Farah" in Aleppo. This elderly home was targeted by Maher and his friends because old people there suffer from disabilities. "I receive support from them now, not the other way round". The challenges are many but to mention only some, Maher stressed the lack of services Aleppo is suffering from, although the situation at the early stages of the war was much worse.

Maher was named by "The Syrian Youth Assembly" to host an online guitar party where anyone can virtually attend in a gesture to spread peace by music. The Syrian Youth Assembly is a platform for young Syrians to work together to build peace. It was set up by a group of Syrian youth who were present at the World Humanitarian Summit in 2016. This initiative is fully youth-led and aims at engaging many Syrian youth around the world. Acceptance from the local host community is key when implementing any project or setting any initiative. Maher reported instances where the same organization would be welcomed by the local community in Aleppo and at the same time severely opposed in Damascus. He attributes the reason for this to the directors of the field offices. Another reason he reports is "the lack of information the local community has on the implemented projects, which leads to misconcep-tions and misinterpretations".

Maher stressed the importance of shedding light on the effect of sanc-tions imposed on the local community. Indeed, locals are in the frontline of those affected by these sanctions. Today, Syrian youth are deprived the right to access major e-learning platforms like Coursera and Duolingo. Added to that is their inability to submit the internationally recognized English language proficiency exams like IELTS and TOEFL. Earlier, they had to cross the border to Lebanon to submit these exams, but now it has become very difficult if not impossible for the majority to do so due to financial restrictions. Every entry to Syria requires them to pay US$100 and for a COVID-19 test.

Conclusion

The slogans carried by the Arab revolutions in early 2011 were mostly led by marginalized youth who had aspirations for a better society. A holistic approach should be initiated in order to avoid social and economic injustices and achieve the political reforms called for. Governments, international organizations, academia, and civil society should tackle existing inequalities and gaps. Improving the economic conditions at first is key and reform must include all members of society. Youth should be recognized not only as recipients, but as the means of change. The presented cases highlight the important role youth play at peacemaking in the Syrian context. In such dire circumstances, they were able to implement great initiatives successfully. This should be an example and proves that youth can make drastic changes when they are determined and enabled. Building proper institutional relations will facilitate this reformation process, especially in a country like Syria where the conflict is protracted, and the current relative stability is expected to be shaken easily. All humanitarian and relief actors inside Syria face challenges with approval processes. Hence, youth initiatives are buried before they are born, and the scene is monopolized by international actors and the local authorities. Lengthy approval processes make it difficult if not impossible sometimes for grassroots initiatives to actualize on the ground.

There are other skills that need to be taken into consideration to increase quality civic engagement among youth. These skills contribute to the making of a more self-motivated youth with enthusiasm for positive change. One of these skills is being mindful of others and being able to sympathize with the weaknesses of the less powerful at the same time as being mindful of yourself, and this can be key when aspiring to resolve conflicts with others. If the youth are taught how to be mindful of themselves, we would witness an elevated state of leadership among them, and this can eventually be reflected in social transformation. By developing awareness of themselves, the youth can deploy this knowledge in two directions at the same time.

- Firstly, they would be able to create and enhance their connections and networks because openness of mind is the first step in fostering relationships. Civil engagement is based on networking and this leads to mobilization.
- Secondly, by developing self-mindfulness the youth will get to know their weaknesses better and will be able to identify areas of competencies that they need to work on more. By being aware of this, the youth will be able to work on their weak areas to develop the organizational skills needed for civic engagement in any organization.

The current Syrian context is not conducive to supporting youth initiatives. More inclusive policies are needed in the Arab world in general, and in Syria specifically, that promote the culture of youth initiatives. Supporting the youth in getting into the labour market through facilitating internships and practical learning opportunities expands the potential for creating more possibilities for them to grow and be more influential in their respective communities. This is done by offering the youth the appropriate support to start building peace from within Syria and not by imposing foreign peace programmes from outside.

References

Aykut, Ö. (2018). *Filling the International and Local Governance Gap in a Presumed 'Failed State': Local Councils in the Opposition-Held Areas of Syria* (Master's thesis, Middle East Technical University).

Battistoni, R. M. (2013). *Civic Learning Through Service Learning: Conceptual Frameworks and Research* (Vol. 1). Retrieved August 2020, from https://scholar .google.com/scholar?as_vis=1&q=battistoni+civic+engagement&hl=en&as_sdt =1,5#aHR0cDovL2Jsb2dzLm10cm95YWwuY2EvaXNvdGwvZmlsZXMvMjA xNi8wNS9jaXZpcYy1sZWFybmluZy5wZGZ.QEAx.

Brown, D., Donini, A., and Knox Clarke, P. (2014) Engagement of crisis-affected people in humanitarian action. Background Paper of ALNAP's. In 29th Annual Meeting, March 11–12, 2014, Addis Ababa. London: ALNAP/ODI.

Crawford, N. (2015). *Engaging with Syrian CSOs. How Can the International Community Engage Better with Syrian Civil Society Organizations during the Civil War.* https://reliefweb.int/report/syrian-arab-republic/engaging-syrian-csos-how-can-international-community-engage-better.

Ekman, J. and Amnå, E. (2012) Political participation and civic engagement: Towards a new typology. *Humaff* 22, 283–300 (2012). https://doi.org/10.2478 /s13374-012-0024-1.

Fioramonti, L. and Heinrich, V. F. (2007). How civil society influences policy. CIVICUS, world alliance for citizen participation. Retrieved August 2020, from *CIVICUS Website*: https://www.civicus.org/view/media/CIVICUS.ODI .Fioramonti.Heinrich.pdf.

Gallup Inc. (2010). *Gallup World Poll.* https://worldview.gallup.com/.

Galtung, J. and Fischer, D. (2013). *Johan Galtung Pioneer of Peace Research* (Vol. 5). Switzerland: Springer. doi:10.1007/978-3-642-32481-9.

Kaldor, Mary. (2003) The idea of global civil society. *International Affairs* 79, No. 3 (2003): 583 –593.

Kawakibi, S. (2012). The paradox of government-organized civil activism in Syria. In P. Aarts and F. Cavatorta, *Civil Society in Syria and Iran: Activism in Authoritarian Contexts* (pp. 169–186). Boulder, CO: Lynne Riener Publishers.

Khalaf, R. (2015). Governance without Government in Syria: Civil society and state building during conflict. *Syria Studies* 7, No. 3 (2015): 37–72.

Khouri, R., Shahida, A., Harb, C., Yassin, N., and Moussa, S. (2011). *A Generation on the Move: Insights into the Conditions, Aspirations, and Activism of Arab Youth*. Youth in the Arab World Issam Fares Institute for Public Policy & International Affairs. Beirut, Lebanon: American University of Beirut.

Levine, P. (2007). Collective action, civic engagement, and the knowledge commons. In C. Hess and E. Ostrom, *Understanding Knowledge as a Commons: From Theory to Practice* (p. 267). London: Massachusetts Institute of Technology. Retrieved August 2020.

Mulderig, M. C. (2013, April). *An Uncertain Future: Youth Frustration and the Arab Spring*. Boston University Frederick S. Pardee Center, 38. Retrieved 2020, from https://open.bu.edu/handle/2144/22677

Paffenholz, T. (2009). *Civil Society and Peacebuilding*. Berlin: The Graduate Institute of International and Development Studies.

Paffenholz, Thania and Christoph Spurk (2006). Civil society, civil engagement and peacebuilding. *Social Development* Papers 36, October 2006. Accessed January 20, 2021, http://hbanaszak.mjr.uw.edu.pl/TempTxt/PaffenholzSpurk_2006_Civil%20Society%20Civic%20Egagement%20and%20Pacebuilding.pdf.

Serwer, D. (2014). *The Role of Civil Society in Syria*. Retrieved January 2021, from peacefare.net: http://www.peacefare.net/?p=19279.

UN (2020). *un.org*. Retrieved from United Nations website: https://www.un.org/en/sections/issues-depth/youth-0/.

UNESCO (2011). *Arab Youth: Civic Engagement and Economic Participation*. Beirut: UNESCO Regional Bureau. Retrieved August 2020, from http://www.unesco.org/new/fileadmin/MULTIMEDIA/FIELD/Beirut/pdf/YCE%20_EN.pdfUnited Nations (2020). World Youth Report. New York. Retrieved 2020, from https://www.un.org/development/desa/youth/wp-content/uploads/sites/21/2020/07/2020-World-Youth-Report-FULL-FINAL.pdf.

6 Young people, "child soldiers," in the post-conflict phase

Peacebuilding challenges

Yousra Hasona

Introduction

Young people aged 15–17 or "child soldiers" are not new to the Arab world; the prevalence of the armed conflict in the Arab Spring countries made the phenomenon very clear. Recruiting children under 18 years (age group 15–17) in the Arab Spring countries is similar to other places. Abduction and force are the main methods the parties use. The hard economic situation and the lack of security are pushing children to join armed groups to survive. Recruiting children in armed conflict is a child rights violation. Children have become an important tool in today's armed conflicts; the UN estimated that the numbers of children who have been recruited were 300,000 in 20 countries worldwide (UN, 2015). The Arab world has witnessed an increase in the number of child soldiers since the 2011 Arab Spring movements. In 2014, a UN report stated that there were 271 cases of child recruitment in Syria, 89 in Somalia, 67 in Iraq, 617 in South Sudan, 6 in Palestine, and 3 in Darfur (Children in Armed Conflict, 2015).

With the uprising of the Arab Spring, the recruitment of children in the Arab countries (Syria, Iraq, Sudan, Libya, and Yemen), either by the state or the armed groups, became more common. This article discusses the impact of the child soldier phenomenon on peace and stability in the Arab Spring countries, and how the Restorative Justice Approach can be used to work with them. Child recruitment consists of: firstly, the child soldiers' age, and secondly, the child soldiers' participation in hostilities. A child is a human being under 18 years of age, as stated by the Convention on the Rights of the Child 1989 (Pedersen and Sommerfelt, 2007). At the national level, many of the Arab countries took the age of 18 for defining the term "child" in their child protection laws. For example, Article 2 from Yemeni Law 2002 concerning Child Rights, Article 4 from the Sudanese Child Law 2010,

Article 1 from the Syrian Juvenile Law 1974, and Article 3 from the Iraqi Juvenile Law 1983 have all set 18 years as the maximum childhood age. However, in many Arab countries, the local cultures do not always stand in line with the law. In Yemen, many tribes deem children's age to be 10; in Sudan male children are considered to be men who are obligated to defend their tribes and work to support their families (Al-Zain, 2020). In addition, the circumstances in many Arab countries, especially after the 2011 Arab Spring, had pushed a massive number of children to participate in hostilities and grow rapidly from childhood to adulthood. Many of the Syrian refugee children in Jordan have returned to Syria to join the armed groups and fight, because they believe that it is their duty to defend their country and their families (Sommerfelt and Taylor, 2015).

Nevertheless, child soldiers' age is still a controversial issue, according to Article 4 of the first Geneva Additional Protocols, and Article 77 of the second Geneva Additional Protocols, the ban on child recruitment is restricted to children under 15 years of age. Age 15 was also adopted by the Convention on the Rights of the Child for child recruitment in Article 38. In the Rome statute, the International Criminal Court (ICC) considered child recruitment under 15 years of age as a war crime (Achvarina and Reich, 2006). On the other hand, both the Cape Town Principles (1977) and the Paris Principles (2007) had adopted the age of 18 years old in their definitions of child soldiers. In addition to that, a lot of international and local NGOs were successful in persuading their international community to recognize the age of 18 as a minimum recruitment age through the Additional Protocol in the Convention of the Rights of the Child adopted in 2002.

Engaging in hostilities

This age group of children (15–17 years old) may play many roles in hostilities, as spies, cooks, bodyguards for the commander, guarding the checkpoint, messengers, and fighters. There is still ongoing debate over the nature of their participation in hostilities. Firstly, *direct participation* in hostilities as defined by the Convention of the Rights of the Child and its additional protocol. Secondly, *active participation* in hostilities as defined by the ICC. The ICC stated that there is no direct and clear difference between the two concepts. Although the Rome statute uses the concept of *actively participating* in Article 2/b/28, the court pointed out in its decision that the concept of active participation is wider than just having a direct relationship in the hostilities (Prosecutor vs Thomas Lubanga Dyilo, 2007). Hence the concept may contain both direct and active participation, for example using children in reconnaissance activities, spying, building traps, using them as human shields, or personal guards, etc. All of these activities can be considered as active participation in the hostilities because they can put the child on the edge of participating directly in the hostilities (Prosecutor vs Fofana and Kondewa, 2007). However, the court adopted a case-by-case approach to deal with what can and what cannot be considered as a form of active participation in hostilities (Prosecutor vs Thomas Lubanga Dyilo, 2007).

The rise of new wars leads to children becoming a major tool to the parties, especially the non-state actors (Achvarina and Reich, 2006). There are two common ways to recruit children, by force, especially through abduction, and voluntary recruitment, when children join the conflict parties by themselves, although it cannot be considered completely voluntary due to the surrounding circumstances like poverty, insecurity, and famine (Wessells, 2005). Most of the children have been abducted from their home, school, or refugee camp by the armed group, and have been forced to train, carry guns, and take a direct part in hostilities (Skinner, 1999). Children are weak and fragile which make them easier to manipulate than adults. They follow orders out of fear, especially with the rough and hard methods they can be exposed to, like physical or mental threats. Another tool many armed groups use to recruit children is cultural and religious models, to ensure children's full loyalty and encourage them to fight (Souris, 2017).

A harsh economic situation like poverty, hunger, and unemployment plays an important role in pushing children to join an armed group to provide food and money for them and their families (Achvarina and Reich, 2006; Brett and Specht, 2004). The lack of security in the conflict areas and the fear of being killed is another reason for children to join armed groups. In other cases, children may be looking for revenge from specific parties which drives them to join the opposite party (Wessells, 2005). A different ideology such as jihadism and nationalism also help the parties to recruit children by force or attract them to join voluntarily. All parties in the Arab Spring countries participate in child recruitment. For instance, ISIS had its special system to recruit children in both Syria and Iraq. The group had its own recruitment system (Morris and Dunning, 2018). ISIS's object was to build a strong Islamic state, to achieve this target they needed a strong and loyal army (Morris and Dunning, 2018).

They focus basically on recruiting children through education; ISIS had its own school system where attendance was compulsory. In the learning curricula of ISIS schools, subjects like art and music were replaced with Quranic, Hadith, and Jihad studies. The children learned how to fight, shoot, and use weapons (Benotman and Malik, 2016: HRW, 2014). Besides ISIS many armed groups recruit children. In Syria, for example, the government forces and the opposition groups such as the Syrian Free Army and Jabhat Al-Nusra, used children in their fight (Sommerfelt and Taylor, 2015; Saleh, 2013). In other places like Somalia and Yemen economics and religion are also reasons for child recruitment. Mainly, Ansar Allah (al-Houthi) in Yemen and al-Shabab in Somalia, use religion as a tool to recruit children (Amnesty, 2011; Child Soldiers, 2017). The Houthi fight is based on their affiliation with the lineage of the Al-AlBayt; therefore they teach children in schools and educational settings that their battle serves the interest of the Houthi right to rule based on the religious authority granted from their lineage (Al-Maliki, 2020). In both countries, the parties push children to join the war and fight for their well-being and safety (Amnesty, 2011; Child Soldiers, 2017).

One of the important factors that should be taken into consideration is that not all of the Arab countries have the same political or sectarian environment. Sectarianism can be a serious issue in Iraq and Syria; in a place like Sudan, child soldiers were used in conflicts over identities and ethnicities between the south and the north (Mayotte, 1994), and over politics and economics which contained conflict over land in Darfur (Al-Zain, 2020). In Syria, children were used from the beginning of the demonstrations. With the revolution going forward they started to engage more in hostilities like providing supplies, carrying weapons, and guarding the checkpoints (Saleh, 2013). In Iraq, ISIS used child soldiers in suicide operations and fighting on the front line (Sommerfelt and Taylor, 2015); many children have been used as human shields, some of them trained to kill people in special units ISIS called *cups of the caliphate,* and some of those children executed people (Almohammad, 2018).

Child soldiers could affect conflict resolution in two ways, the continuation of the war and social instabilities. Children in Arab Spring countries are a broad category, and re-recruiting them from one armed group to another means that the war engine will continue to spin and keep on going. For instance, many child soldiers who get demobilized in South Sudan have been re-recruited in the fight (UN, Children in Armed Conflict, 2016). Another way to keep the conflict moving is child soldiers keeping their weapons and using violence as a way to survive, especially when they do not have alternative solutions (Fanthorpe and Maconachie, 2010).

Many of the Berber children who joined the Libyan revolution and fought alongside the National Transitional Council were left behind, and they were accused of drinking or having HIV (Amusan, 2013). These children started looking for other opportunities and some of them found it within the jihadist groups in Libya, and others used weapons and violence as a way to survive (Amusan, 2013). Similarly, a huge number of Sudanese soldiers including former child soldiers are fighting in Yemen for one or more parties (Al-Zain, 2020). At some point, some children become racist, and killers. They commit crimes against others who are different from them

(Morris and Dunning, 2018). As a result, people in Iraq look down on them, refuse to deal with them, or have them back among the community (Mousa, 2020; Subhan, 2020).

Another factor related to the social context is the effect of recruitment on children themselves. Child soldiers suffer from emotional and psychological consequences, such as Post Traumatic Stress Disorder, stress, fear, nightmare, and anxiety (Schauer and Elbert, 2010; Johannessen and Holgersen, 2014). This controls how children communicate with their surroundings, they start avoiding people, isolate themselves, and in some cases, it could turn violent (Ozerdem and Podder, 2011). ISIS child soldiers, who went back to their families refused to stay with them in the beginning, and some children used violence against their family members or properties (Dozier, 2019).

In different cases, children had difficulties with returning to civil life, and rebuilding their relationship with the community through an integration process.

Reintegration process

This process aims to contribute to security and stability in the post-war phase through rehabilitation and reintegration. The rehabilitation process contains two main parts. The first is healthcare as many child soldiers suffer from many physical and psychological injuries, which leave them vulnerable in civilian life (Mahmood, 2016). The second is training and education programmes and to provide them with the necessary skills to help them get involved in the labour market (Skinner, 1999). This will help children to find a job and support themselves rather than relying on military groups as a source of money and food (Betancourt, 2008). Although disarmament, demobilization, and reintegration (DDR) programmes are not new in Arab countries, they face many difficulties when it comes to child soldiers. The NGOs which work on those DDR programmes face many problems, such as in Iraq – the huge number of children, the funding difficulties compared to the growing needs, government ignorance, and late intervention (Subhan, 2020; Mousa, 2020).

In Yemen, the state and the people are not even thinking about DDR, for the local community the peace for them is so far away, so DDR is not a priority (Al-Maliki, 2020). In similar thinking, the child soldiers in Sudan are a source of pride to their tribes, hence, fighting is necessary to survive, which means leaving the DDR programmes out of the children's and communities' consideration (Al-Zain, 2020). However, reintegration is "a long complex process that is as much about helping children find an appropriate social place as it is about individual rehabilitation" (Wessells, 2005, p. 366). In this phase, the main consideration is to return the children to their community once again, as a way to rebuild their social identities and help them become part of the community. In some cases, children face rejection and stigmatization by society due to the crimes and human rights violations they committed, and the conflict parties they fought for (Bloom and Beha, 2017).

One of the main problems that faces children who fight or accompany ISIS in Iraq is social rejection, isolation, and in some cases the demands to kill them or send them out of the country (Subhan, 2020; Mousa, 2020). The reason behind this is the crimes those children committed, or simply because they were part of ISIS (Subhan, 2020; Mousa, 2020). However, it should be noted that the social rejection level is related to the conflict itself. While in Iraq the community is against ISIS children, in Yemen and Sudan the society is more accepting, due to the fact that those children are fighting for their communities and not foreign groups (Al-Zain, 2020; Al-Maliki, 2020). In the Arab Spring countries, child soldiers are being arrested instead of reintegrated through DDR programmes. As reported by the UN Secretary General in 2018, 902 Iraqi children were in detention due to national security issues related to their relationship with armed groups like ISIS. In Somalia, almost 375 children are still imprisoned by the Somali National Army and other armed groups (UN, 2019).

Keeping child soldiers in jail without trial, or even prosecuting them as criminals under the criminal law will not help in bringing the community and victims the justice they demand, or rehabilitate and reintegrate the children into the community. For the purpose of building a balance between the victims' and child soldiers' rights, an approach like Restorative Justice (RJ) can be more suitable than prosecuting them.

Restorative justice (RJ)

RJ is a method to use in criminal matters to achieve justice in a different way than standard criminal justice. Its aim is to bring the offender, the victim, and the community together. It also attempts to address the offender's criminal responsibility for his wrongdoing and to recognize the victim's pain from those actions (Braithwaite, 2011; Barsky, 2017; Duff, 2011). Walgrave and Bazemore define RJ as "every action that is primarily oriented toward doing justice by repairing the harm that has been caused by a crime" (Walgrave, 2001, p. 18). The main consideration is the harm that the crime left, thus the aim should be focussed more on restoring the harm, and not what should be done to the offender (Walgrave, 2004), while Tony Marshall defines RJ as a "process whereby the parties with a stake in a particular offence come together to resolve collectively how to deal with the aftermath of the offence and its implications for the future" (Crawford and Newburn, 2003, p. 22). Marshall does not require that the process outcomes should be restorative and at the same time he does not consider practices that exclude one party as a restorative practice (Walgrave, 2004, p. 552). In her vision for RJ, Susan Sharpe presents a number of features for the RJ process (Ness et al., 2001, pp. 5–6). The most general description for RJ came from Braithwaite who describes it as, "whatever dimensions matter to the victims, offenders and communities affected by the crime" (Crawford and Newburn, 2003, p. 23).

The point of using RJ instead of the normal criminal justice in the case of juveniles, especially child soldiers, can achieve two main objectives. The first is helping the children themselves to understand the wrong they did and the harm they caused to the community through admitting their responsibility. The second is helping the victim and community in understanding why and under what circumstances the children did those actions. The most important outcome for RJ is to reintegrate child soldiers within the community, as well as to bring the victim closer to forgiving and welcoming those children among them. This can reflect positively on the reconciliation between the children, the victims, and the community (Zehr and Gohar, 2003; Huyneh, et al., 2015; Llewellyn, 2006).

NGOs play essential role in raising people's awareness of what happened to those children, how were they abducted, what they faced during the war, and how the armed groups used them and forced them to commit the crimes (Williamson, 2006). In a more organized and governmental framework, East Timor had an effective programme closer to RJ, called the Community Reconciliation Processes (CRPs), which was part of the Commission for Reception, Truth, and Reconciliation (CAVR) work (Burgess, 2006). The programme aimed to prosecute the perpetrators who committed crimes or worked with the Indonesians in general. The CRPs were voluntarily programmed which helped in attracting a lot of perpetrators, and it used the traditional ways and norms in prosecuting those perpetrators by the community members (Burgess, 2006; Pigou, 2004). Many of the perpetrators who went through this process received community forgiveness by admitting what they did was wrong and apologizing; some of them got some sanction but it was not hard punishment, and in the end, the community welcomed them back (Pigou, 2004).

RJ is not prosecuting child soldiers, but healing victims' pain through listening to the children apologize for the wrong they have done. This process will help the victims in understanding, accepting, and maybe forgiving which can lead to more stability and assure both the victim and the children's rights. Back in the 1980s when the war in Afghanistan against the Soviet Union was over, no Arab countries accepted Arab jihadists who had fought there. Although Saudi Arabia was the main sponsor for them, it refused to deal with any of them. Additionally, countries like Egypt and Saudi Arabia did not have any DDR programmes; they either arrested those fighters or refused to let them back into the country. The result of that was the start of a new wave of violence; new armed groups emerged and fought in different places like Algeria and Bosnia and Herzegovina (Atteridge, 2016; Macdonald, 2019). In a similar situation, most of the Arab Spring countries today like Iraq, Syria, Libya, Sudan, and Yemen do not have any plans for DDR programmes for either adults or for children (Al-Zain, 2020; Al-Maliki, 2020; Mousa, 2020; Subhan, 2020).

The Arab Spring countries need to focus on creating special programmes under the general framework of RJ for child soldiers that aim to help them reintegrate into the community and build new understanding of the role of both children and victims in the healing and reconciliation process in the post-conflict phase. Although DDR has the same goal, RJ is one step ahead. Based on this study, the programme has two phases. The first one should focus on how children will reconcile with themselves. Much work should be done on accepting themselves and others, and helping the children adjust to civilian life. In this stage, the children's families should have a supportive role to help their children in moving on, and understanding what they went through, and how they can move on and start a new life.

The second phase is about reconciling child soldiers with their victims and communities. Through the first phase, the children should know what is wrong in what they learned and did, which will reflect on their relationship with their society. The community itself needs to listen to those children admit that what they did was harmful and apologize for the damage they caused. This will help the victims to accept and forgive; as a result the community's ability to turn a new page with them will grow. Through RJ, the children, the victims, and the community will have to come to an agreement at the end of the process. So instead of prison punishment, the parties can choose to do different things, like community service, helping build homes and schools, or cleaning streets and gardens. The main objective is pushing children to participate in the reconstruction, which will strengthen their feeling of belonging within the community and will help society to look at them in a different light other than as fighters and criminals.

Conclusion

Child soldiers are a phenomenon that should not be ignored in the Arab region, and these children should be treated neither as criminals nor as unwanted members of society. The recruitment of children in Arab countries is one of the most prominent tools that is used by the conflict parties, and with the continuation of the fighting children are still forced to participate in hostilities directly or indirectly, they may be used as guards or fighters, which can affect their relationship with their societies, especially when committing human rights violations against the community members.

The DDR programmes are the first step to work with child soldiers, but many Arab countries are facing problems with these programmes, which reflects negatively on their effectiveness, and therefore RJ is one of the mechanisms that can help to look at the issue of child soldiers more broadly. The main idea around RJ is creating a balance between the child soldiers' right to reintegrate into the society, and the victim's right to have justice, it will help create a strong platform capable of being the core to a sustainable conflict resolution process which consequently leads to sustainable peace and stability.

The governments should start looking into how it can integrate RJ programmes for child soldiers into the general plans of the Ministries of Justice. The first step is to establish a special commission with its main aim to create a suitable plan for the community, taking into consideration the social, economic, security, political, and justice needs. And how can RJ help fulfil those aspects, in order to achieve both children's and society's interest. The government's strategy must also include a sufficient number of workers on this project, particularly those with legal backgrounds such as lawyers, judges, mostly from the juvenile justice and childcare departments. It also should work on qualifying them on being part of both monitoring and implementing the RJ programmes with child soldiers. The government must also study the best means to reduce the victims' pain in a way the children themselves can be part of. These pre-studies are the best way to ensure that the sessions will be able to merge society's and the children's needs without favouring one party over another.

One of the main issues the governments must pay attention to is how tribes, clans, NGOs, and CSOs can be included in the programmes. For example, governments can use NGOs and CSOs to educate communities about child soldiers and start awareness campaigns to remove the mistaken and negative image that societies have about child soldiers. Those activities can be a helpful tool that contributes to preparing the community members to look differently at those children before the second phase starts. The role that tribes and clans can play in helping the governments succeed in implementing these projects is huge, especially with the fact that Arab societies still rely heavily on them. The most important role is the clans' and the tribes' ability to persuade local communities to engage in these programmes and cooperate through joining those meetings. Another one is the ability to facilitate holding sessions between children and the community members and also providing assistance in places which could be difficult for the government to reach. They can also help in the implementation of the programme outputs, from supporting the children within the community, to obliging the local communities with the outcomes.

References

Achvarina, V. and Reich, S. (2006). No Place to Hide: Refugees, Displaced Persons, and the Recruitment of Child Soldiers. *International Security*, 128 *31* (1), 127–164.

Al-Maliki, J. (2020). *Researcher and film producer for Al-Jazeera Media Network* (Y. Hasona, Interviewer) Doha.

Almohammad, A. (2018). *ISIS Child Soldiers in Syria: The Structural and Predatory Recruitment, Enlistment, Pre-Training Indoctrination, Training, and Deployment*. International Center for Counter-Terrorim.

Al-Zain, S.-D. (2020). *Director of Al Jazeera Center for Studies*. (Y. Hassoune, Interviewer). Doha.

Amnesty. (2011). *In the Line of Fire: Somalia's Children under Attack*. London: Amnesty International.

Amusan, L. (2013). Libya's Implosion and Its Impacts on Children. *Journal of International Women's Studies*, *14* (5),66–79.

Atteridge, A. (2016). *Foreign Fighters Post Conflict: Assessing the Impact of Arab Afghans and Syrian-Iraqi Foreign Fighters on Global Security*. International Institute for Counter-Terrorism.

Barsky, A. (2017). *Conflict Resolution for the Helping Professions*. Oxford: Oxford University Press.

Benotman, N. and Malik, N. (2016). *The Children of Islamic State*. London: Quilliam.

Betancourt, T. (2008). High Hopes, Grim Reality: Reintegration and the Education of Former Child Soldiers in Sierra Leone. *Comparative Education Review*, *52* (4), 565–587. doi: 10.1086/591298.

Bloom, M. and Beah, I. (2017). *Cubs to Lions: What's Next for ISIL's Child Soldiers?* Retrieved February 29, 2020, from aljazrrea:https://www.aljazeera.com/indepth/features/2017/11/cubs-lions-isil-child-soldiers-171109125013897.html.

Braithwaite, J. (2011). In Search of Restorative Jurisprudence. In M. Tonry (Ed.), *Why Punish? How much?*. Oxford: Oxford University Press.

Brett, R. and Specht, I. (2004). *Young Soldiers, Why They Choose to Fight*. Boulder, CO: Lynne Rienner Publishers.

Burgess, P. (2006). A New Approach to Restorative Justice: East Timor Community Reconciliation Processes. In N. Roht-Arriaza (Ed.), *Transitional Justice in the Twenty-First Century*. Cambridge: Cambridge University Press.

ChildSoldiers (2017). *Yemen Country Report: Children and Security*. The Romeo Dallaire Child Soldiers Initiative. https://www.dallaireinstitute.org/wp-content/uploads/2020/01/RDCSI_AnnualReport_2017_14x8-5_V6_full_web.pdf.

Crawford, Adam and Newburn, Tim (2003). *Youth Offending and Restorative Justice: Implementing Reform in Youth Justice*. Devon: WILLAN.

Dozier, K. (2019). *They Were Children When They Were Kidnapped By ISIS and Forced to Fight. What Happens Now That They're Home?* Retrieved February 27, 2020, from TIME: https://time.com/longform/isis-child-soldiers-yezidi/.

Duff, R. (2011). Restorative Punishment and Punitive Restoration. In M. Tonry, *Why Punish? How much?* Oxford: Oxford University Press.

Fanthorpe, R. and Maconachie, R. (2010). Beyond the Crisis of Youth? Mining, Farming and Civil Society in Post-War Sierra Leone. *African Affairs, 109* (435), 251–272.

General-Secretary (2016). *Children in Armed Conflict.* New York: United Nation.

General-Secretary (2015). *Children in Armed Conflict.* New York: United Nation.

Human Rights Watch (HRW). (2014). *Maybe we Live and Maybe we Die.* New York: Human Rights Watch.

Huyneh, K. et al. (2015). *Children and Global Conflict.* Cambridge: Cambridge University Press.

Johannessen, S. and Holgersen, H.(2014). Former Child Soldiers' Problems and Needs: Congolese Experiences. *Qualitative Health Research, 24* (1), 55–66.

Llewellyn, J. (2006). Restorative Justice in Transition and Beyond: The Justice Potential of Truth-Telling Mechanisms for Post-Peace Accord Societies. In T. Borer (Ed.), *Telling the Truths: Truth Telling and Peace Building in Post-Conflict Societies.* Notre Dame, IN: Notre Dame University.

Macdonald, M. (2019). *Why Did It All Go So Wrong? An Arab Veteran of the Anti-Soviet Jihad Speaks.* Retrieved 2 29, 2020, from War on Rocks: https://warontherocks.com/2019/03/why-did-it-all-go-so-wrong-an-arab-veteran-of-the-anti-soviet-jihad-speaks/.

Mahmood, S. (2016). "Cubs of Caliphate": The Islamic States Focus on Children. *Counter Terrorist Trend and Analyses, 8* (10).

Mayotte, J. (1994). The Paradox of Human Rights and National Sovereignty. *Journal of International Affairs Editorial Board, 47* (2), 497–524.

Morris, J. and Dunning, T. (2018). Rearing Cubs of the Caliphate: An Examination of Child Soldier Recruitment by Da'esh. *Terrorism and Political Violence.*

Mousa, H. (2020). *Professor of International Relations* (Y. Hasona, Interviewer). College of Political Science, University of Mosul.

Ness, D, Morris, A, and Maxwell, G. (2001). Introducing Restorative Justice. In A. M. Maxwell (Ed.), *Restorative Justice For Juveniles.* Oxford: HART Publishing.

Ozerdem, A. and Podder, S. (2011). *Child Soldiers: From Recruitment to Reintegration.* New York: Palgrave Macmillan.

Pedersen, J. and Sommerfelt, T. (2007). Studying Children in Armed Conflict: Data Production, Social Indicators and Analysis. *Social Indicators Research,* 255–256.

Pigou, P. (2004). *The Community Reconciliation Process of the Commission for Reception, Truth and Reconciliation.* Timor-Leste: UNDP.

Prosecutor vs Monina Fofana and Allieu Kondewa, Judgment, SCSL -04–14-1, 2 (SCSL August 2007).

Prosecutor vs Thomas Lubanga Dyilo, Decision on the confirmation of charges, 01/04-01/06 (ICC January 29, 2007).

Saleh, L. (2013). "We Thought We Were Playing": Children's Participation in the Syrian Revolution. *Journal of International Women's Studies*, *14* (5), 80–95.

Schauer, E. and Elbert, T. (2010). The Psychological Impact of Child Soldiering. In E. Martz (Ed.), *Trauma Rehabilitation After War and Conflict* (pp. 312–360). New York: Springer.

Skinner, P. (1999). Child Soldiers in Africa: A Disaster for Future Families. *International Journal on World Peace*, *9*.

Sommerfelt, T. and Taylor, M. (2015). *The Big Dilemma of Small Soldiers: Recruiting Children to the War in Syria*. Norwegian Peacebuilding Resource Center.

Souris, N. (2017). Child Soldiering on Trial: An Interdisciplinary Analysis of Responsibility in the Lord's Resistance Army. *International Journal of Law in Context*, 323–324.

Subhan, A. (2020). *Professor at the College of Political Science* (Y. Hasona, Interviewer). University of Mosul.

UN (2015). *4 Out of 10 Child Soldiers Are Girls*. Retrieved March 23, 2020, from Office of the Secretary-General's Envoy on Youth: https://www.un.org/youthenvoy/2015/02/4-10-child-soldiers-girls/.

UN (2019). *Children and Armed Conflict in Yemen*. New York: United Nations Secretary-General.

Walgrave, L. (2001). On Restoration and Punishment: Favourable Similarities and Fortunate Differences. In A. M. Maxwell (Ed.), *Restorative Justice For Juveniles*. Oxford: HART Publishing.

Walgrave, L. (2004). Restoration in Youth Justice. *Crime and Justice*, *31*, 543–597.

Wessells, M. (2005). Child Soldiers, Peace Education, and Postconflict Reconstruction for Peace. *Theory Into Practice*, 364.

Williamson, J. (2006). The Disarmament, Demobilization and Reintegration of Child Soldiers: Social and Psychological Transformation in Sierra Leone. *Intervention*, *4* (3), 158–205.

Zehr, H. and Gohar, A. (2003). *The Little Book of Restorative Justice*.010234930Information   Classification: General00Information Classification: General

7 Young women's involvement in the Yemeni conflict

New roles in a changing environment

Abdulrahman Abohajeb, Belal Abdo, and Ala Mohsen

Introduction

The 2011 uprisings in the Arab world have unleashed significant social and political change in the region (Beck and Hüser, 2012). In Yemen, peaceful rallies led by women and young people to confront the authoritarian regime marked the beginning of social transformation in respect of increased female activism in the country (Alwazir, 2016). A subsequent surge in young women's participation during the transition process supports the notion of political and social transformation. In the National Dialogue Conference (NDC), which provided a platform to discuss visions for a new Yemen, scenes of women arguing with well-known sheikhs indicated a breakaway from an era of marginalization that subdued Yemeni women (Hennessey, 2015). Unfortunately, the transition process failed, and the war broke out between the parties that were involved in the NDC.

As war leaves its impact on different aspects, it also assigns new roles to women in response to new developments, thus allowing new players (e.g., Houthi women) to dominate other women in the country (TOBE Foundation, 2017). This chapter elaborates on one such specific aspect of transformation: the militarization and mobilization of armed Houthi women – *Al-Zainabiyat*, tracing the factors through which we can explain the new trend of women's mobilization and militarization in Yemen.

Women in northern Yemen: an overview

Prior to the wave of Islamization that hit Yemen during the 1980s and 1990s, rural Yemeni women used to be more visible in the public space. For instance, they used to dance with men, have their own businesses in local markets, and travel without an escort, etc. (Adra, 2016, p. 320). As

Wahhabism spread across Yemen, Islamists contested the public visibility of women and considered it a wrongdoing that violates the rules set by religion. For example, propositions such as "when a man is in seclusion with a woman, their third partner is the devil" instil the idea of inevitable sexual attraction and thus calls for the suppression of all means that invoke "impure" sexual desire (Zanelli, 2013). The state apparatus has also facilitated such segregation through the educational curricula and schools' classrooms, creating boys-only and girls-only schools and classrooms as an official policy (Abohajeb personal communication, 2020).

The conservative Islah Party has enjoyed much leverage in designing the educational curricula, and therefore, enforcing the party's conservative principles and agendas. The phenomenon of gender segregation has been seen widely across Yemen. Depending on whether the women live in urban or rural areas, the extent of such segregation has varied based on the level of penetration by external influences. According to an old study carried out by Buringa (1988, pp. 43–45), prior to the wave of Islamization, women in rural areas enjoyed greater autonomy with more visible mobility and economic participation relative to their urban counterparts. Urbanization and Islamization have been a pivotal game changer in the status of women in Yemen. Both have radically reshaped the roles of women and affected their mobility and visibility. The increasing gender segregation in all spheres has thus limited women's participation in the public space (Strzelecka, 2013: para 28).

In rural areas, urbanization brought strangers that could not be trusted as they may do harm to women. Consequently, Yemeni men and women have become more segregated than before, unless they are family and village members (Buringa 1988, p. 41). Moreover, under the pressure of Islamists who enjoyed significant political influence, especially after the 1993 parliamentary elections, the government adopted certain policies that reinforced gender segregation. For example, except at primary and higher education levels, boys and girls attend gender-based schools with mostly female teachers teaching girls and male teachers teaching boys. The state-sanctioned segregation policies increased in momentum and contributed further to the increasing invisibility of women. Simultaneously, the tribal order has also been changed, and women became further confined to their households. Their participation has seldom existed. They could be neither tribal nor community leaders, which in a way reinforced societal/social conservatism. As a result, women have become more dependent on men to represent their legal, economic, and political rights more than ever before (Weir, 2007, pp. 45–51), which is in stark contradiction with the Yemeni constitution.

According to the Yemeni constitution, women and men enjoy the same rights and duties (Buringa, 1988, p. 56). Since democracy was introduced in northern Yemen, women and men have had equal rights in voting and competing in elections (ibid.). In the post-unification parliamentary election of 1993, 21 women ran for seats, however only two of them entered the parliament (ibid.). The number of women candidates increased in subsequent elections. In the first local council elections in 2001, among the 147 women who ran in the election, 38 women secured seats (National Democratic Institute, 2003, p. 30). Nevertheless, female representation remained low despite the doubling of the number of women voters from 1.8 million in 1997 to 3.4 million in 2001. Scholars have tried to explain the reason behind the low representation of women as due to fear of impropriety to attract attention in public spaces (Buringa, 1988, p. 51). As society looks down on women's visibility and their active participation in the public sphere, women are somehow forced to choose between either family life or public life. Subsequently, women usually prefer the private secluded lifestyle to guarantee prospects for marriage and family-making (Adra, 2010, pp. 8–9).

The 2011 youth revolution and beyond

For the first time in decades, the 2011 youth revolution brought back men and women together in public gatherings. Dismantling gender segregation was one of the impressive sociocultural achievements of Yemen's peaceful youth uprising. In Maydan al-Tagheer, "Change Square," women were enthusiastic participants in the protests – playing leading roles in organizing and coordinating different activities in the square and beyond (Al-Sakkaf 2012, p. 1). The call for women's active participation during the crisis was embedded in Yemeni culture. Oral narratives or folk tales that older people communicate to the younger generation explain women's role in resisting authoritarian rulers of Yemeni old kingdoms (Taibah and MacDonald, 2015, pp. 71–75). The stories of Yemeni women revolting against kings who reigned through terror and injustice inspired the younger generation to be more justice-oriented and become more active in public affairs/life. In these stories, a brave and wise woman steps up and deposes the oppressive corrupt king, took his place as a queen and led the kingdom towards stability and prosperity. Such kinds of narrative passed from one generation to another, empowering Yemeni women, which explains why women took the lead in the 2011 revolution. The Nobel laureate Tawakkol Karman, with other female figures, led and organized protests and demonstrations against Saleh's regime (Adra, 2016, p. 317). Most people in Yemen cheered Karman's leadership and some argued that she reminded them of their famous Queen of Sheba and the great kingdom she ruled (Finn, 2015). In fact, Yemeni women became politically visible thanks to their active participation in the revolution during 2011 and beyond.

Another explanation for women's active role in the revolution comes from the tribal customary law in Yemen (Adra, 2016, p. 317). The customary law entrusts women with the role of mediating and settling tribal disputes and running tribal affairs (Adra 2010, p. 8). Additionally, the tribal customary law is a culture-based legal system that protects women and marginalized groups (ibid.). For this purpose, a significant number of tribesmen marched into cities to protect young men and women demonstrators from harm and incursions of government forces (Adra, 2016, p. 319). The fact that tribesmen joined the protesting youths in their demonstrations was surprising for many foreign observers as tribal men are known to carry guns at all times. It was no ordinary scene to see those tribesmen leaving their arms at home to take part in peaceful protests.

Prior to the youth revolution, the mobilization of women was to some extent rare. Among these rare occasions, political parties used to mobilize women in order to challenge the status quo and force the governing regime to negotiate and compromise, particularly prior to local, parliamentary and presidential elections. This kind of mobilization was politically driven and occurred only when mobilizing men became difficult and dangerous. In fact, the weaker side of the conflicting parties tends to mobilize women against its opponents in an attempt to destroy their reputation and turn the public against its opponent. The ruling regime calculates the consequences of any violent response against protesting women. This is what happened during the regime's attempt to crack down on a women's protest in 2011. As the regime responded with violence, the tribal community and Yemeni people reacted to the women's appeal for support and protection. Also, political parties benefitted from mobilizing women to gain Western support for these protests. The Western media has portrayed the Yemeni women's uprising as a positive transformation of Yemen's society towards greater female participation in the public sphere, which added legitimacy to the protests.

Following the onset of civil war in 2015, a new phenomenon of women's participation has emerged in the new context of war (UNDP, 2017). A recent encounter between peaceful women protesters and armed female militia shocked Yemenis. A group of Houthi women calling themselves "*Al-Zainabiyat*" i.e., Patrons of Zainab, led a violent crackdown of female protesters who gathered to demand the handover of the former president's body – Saleh's body (Snyder, 2017). The scene of female militants carrying sticks, and sometimes armed, and beating marching women to suppress their protest has been an unprecedented phenomenon in Yemeni society. The incident was seen as a violation of the customary law and tribal norms and values that protect women from any violence, let alone being perpetrators of violence themselves. Moreover, beating women is a morally abhorrent act in a society that portrays women as innocent yet vulnerable souls that need to be protected.

Al-Zainabiyat: the all-women Houthi militia faction

The Al-Zainabiyat are named after the granddaughter of Muslim prophet Mohammed – Zainab. The same Zainab is also the daughter of prophet Mohammed's cousin Ali bin Abi Talib – a controversial Muslim figure strongly believed by Shia Muslims as the true appointed successor (caliph) of the Prophet Mohammed. Those who identify themselves as "Zainabiyat" (plural) / "Zainabiyya" (singular) uphold the exact identity of Houthi women. In interviews with a group of women who identified themselves as Zainabiyat, the interviewees revealed two opposing views and understandings on the make-up of the Al-Zainabiyat. One group of interviewees said that all female members of Hashemite families (descendants of the Muslim prophet Mohammed) are by nature Zainabiyat. The second group of women – members of a Houthi armed group that hail from native tribes of Yemen – said that any woman who takes Zainab's virtues of chastity, morality, patience, modesty, and jihad, embodies her great role in committing to religion as her way of life and fulfils her duties of worship, prayer, and faith is considered "Zainabiyya" without necessarily being Hashemite.

They all concurred that Al-Zainabiyat – as widely recognized in Yemen – are armed battalions of all-female members which is part of the Houthi movement armed group that has been active since the Houthis' takeover of Yemen's capital Sana'a in March 2015. The Al-Zainabiyat battalion is known to be an indispensable faction of the Houthi militia structure. They take on various roles ranging from indoctrination to mobilization activities including intelligence, security, and military operations (UNSC, 2020, p. 10). This faction carries out different acts that serve the group agenda. The Al-Zainabiyat have committed gross human rights abuses and violations against men, women, families, and tribal communities as part of the Houthi's efforts to sustain its grip on the areas it controls (UNSC, 2020, p. 10). However, the Al-Zainabiyat did not come to existence recently. Hussein Al-Houthi established "the Believing Youth" group in the early 1990s, which later became identified as a Houthi armed group and now calls itself "Ansarullah" (Palik, 2017, p. 49), and the Al-Zainabiyat came under its authority. The Ansarullah is linked to and directed by Iranian supreme leader Ali Khamenei who is also believed to be leading the Hashemite international political organization.

Violence and the issue of gender protection

In 2011, after the Yemeni regime security forces tried to disperse a group of female protesters with water cannons, the incident was immediately condemned by tribal confederations who consequently sent tribesmen to protect those women (Jubran, 2011). Prior to this incident, a Houthi-affiliate Yemeni activist Ali Albukhiti was beaten by Houthi women (or Al-Zainabiyat) as he protested against the movement in attempt to release political detainees. He could not fight back or defend himself as Yemeni customary law prohibited him from responding to women. For this reason, the Houthis sent their women to beat him and in case he fought back, the armed men would beat him up as the customary law allows them to do. This complex tradition in Yemen was supposedly established to preserve honour, dignity, and the rights of all. According to customary law, women should be respected, and protected from any violence at all times (Jubran, 2011). However, the actions of Houthi women demonstrate their lack of respect and disregard for customary law, and most importantly, for human rights. If one asks Yemenis who are not affiliated with Houthis, the answer would be the movement and its overall actions, especially the actions of Houthi women, which are abhorrent to Yemen and its customs and traditions.

Overall, the Yemenis strongly argue that Houthis are Hashemites – decedents of the Prophet Mohammed who came to Yemen seeking refuge, protection, and escape from prosecution by ruling elites in what is known today as Saudi Arabia. As Arab Muslims with strong values that stress helping those in distress, the Yemenis embraced the Hashemites and welcomed them initially as mediators of tribal conflicts and eventually as leaders. As a result, the Hashemites established various dynasties that ruled many different parts of Yemen for centuries until the Republican Revolution ended the Hamidaddin Imamate rule in 1962 (Al-Nu'man, 2018). The Houthis are seen as an extension of the imamate era and are accused of seeking to restore the old regime. Houthis utilize religion to gain the hearts and minds of uneducated Yemenis. However, these precarious moves of Houthis might lead to the marginalization of Hashemites at the end of this war. Yemenis' disapproval of Hashemites has lately increased as result of Houthi violence and violation of all customary laws that protect vulnerable men and women. One might also argue that the activities of Houthi women have disrupted the established customary norms that discourage women from overt participation in political violence. Still, the extreme actions of Houthis and their women stem from the fear of losing what they have gained, but paradoxically, this only increases hatred toward them. Similarly, Hashemites consider themselves "superior" to others because of their descent, esoteric religious education, roles in the imamate state, and linkage to the prophet (Weir 2007, pp. 52–55).

In the last decades, Yemeni women have started to serve as judges, police and military officers, governmental officials, and elected members of parliament and local councils. Furthermore, despite the progress made to include women in the armed security forces and governmental institutions, women are, however, still largely underrepresented in the public sector. As Yemeni women took leading roles in the revolution that toppled a 33-year-old regime, it was expected that women would play a more active role in the post-2011 period. However, the actions of the Al-Zainabiyat undermined the progress that Yemeni women have made so far as they deviated from the peaceful roles women have traditionally subscribed to. The problem of the Al-Zainabiyat lies in their actions toward society as whole. They are religiously oriented and driven as they tend to chant a sectarian slogan that portrays them as extremist offenders rather than victims (Al Arabiya, 2017a). Changing roles at the time of war have enabled women to disregard social norms that excluded them from some space in public affairs but are perceived to be Islamically acceptable. A video of an armed Houthi women's rally explains through their public exercise the religious motivations of their actions (The Jerusalem Post, 2015). Hidden behind the black dress of a long cloak and the niqab (Al Arabiya, 2017b) that covers all their body, while holding guns and chanting violent slogans, is reminiscent of terrorist groups such as ISIS.

The tasks carried out by these women include both indirect and direct involvement in the battle. While some women send their children to fight alongside Houthis, others collect money, and make food and clothes for combatants; other women are extremely active with the operations of planting mines and providing logistics and intelligence for combatants (The Baghdad Post, 2017). As the Hadi-loyal forces approach Houthi-controlled areas, women will become combatants as well. They have been trained how to use guns and how to fight in cities. While anti-Houthi countries, especially the Gulf States, claim that Houthi women (Al-Zainabiyat) have been forced to carry out recruitment and militarization, some observers admit this phenomenon is voluntary and religiously driven. Houthi men and women fight with whatever means to restore their imamate legacy, which ruled most of northern part of Yemen and the southern parts of the Saudi kingdom for over ten centuries.

Even though Houthis have been mobilizing women to crack down on other women, lately Houthi armed women (Al-Zainabiyat) have violently crushed male protesters as well. Incidents of physical violence against women circulates social media with condemnation from local and international organizations (Al-Arab, 2018). The point here is the differential treatment for women and the over-emphasis on their honour, dignity, and considering women as vulnerable human beings, has led to their marginalization. The Houthis, however, are changing this depiction of women with their violations of human rights. Women who refuse to obey Houthis are not spared beating, rape, or death and this indicates a change in the agents of protection, as men used to protect their families and now the women do so. The explanation of the Houthis' actions stems from their belief in social categorization and hierarchization. Hashemites (Houthis) consider themselves to be above others; their women are honourable while other women are not, their bloodline is holy while others' is not (Addin, 2016, p. 1). In fact, women were not even thought to be capable of committing violence and they were rather perceived as "vulnerable," thus it is not honourable for men to abuse weak individuals, including women. Secondly, according to customary law, women represent more than themselves – that is the honour of their families, tribes, and society at large (Abohajeb personal communication, 2020).

Women countering oppression and violence

In defiance of Houthi authority, tribal and rural women take a leading role in conflict mediation and resolution in tribal areas. There are reports of increased female involvement in peacebuilding and conflict resolution. Sumaya Al-Hussam, a Yemeni activist, has succeeded in resolving a blood feud between two tribes that lasted for 11 years. The role of women in conflict resolution is only one example of the many positive roles that women play in society. If the history of Yemen is examined, it is found that Yemeni women have played a crucial role in resolving conflicts, assisting men or sheikhs to gain in-depth knowledge of the problem in hand (Adra, 2016, p. 316). Adra elaborated on the role that women play in disputes and how they use children as messengers between men and women, thus, transferring the opinions of wives and husbands. As sheikhs are sidelined under Houthi authority, women express defiance of Houthi authority through their newly acquired roles that were until recently dominated by sheikhs. According to focus group discussions (2020), women settle disputes internally before reaching a level where the Houthis will interfere. This vacuum resulted from the sheikhs' weakness to defy Houthi authority and thus produced a new generation of "behind closed doors" women leaders who engage in traditional conflict resolution. Women who recognize the critical situation and enjoy a respectable reputation intervene and consult knowledgeable sheikhs on tribal customary law to resolve emerging disputes. Additionally, women in Houthi-controlled areas work in local markets as tailors, selling goods and clothes to provide for their families. However, the Al-Zainabiyat are keeping them at bay.

In government-controlled areas, women stand up to the government soldiers and prevent violations of captured child fighters. They provide significant care in rehabilitating those children who were recruited and brainwashed by the Houthis to fight against government forces. A recent study by Saferworld (Heinze, 2017, p. 19) highlighted a dual role of women as contributors to the war effort and as peacebuilders. The ascent of Houthi women raises another perspective of Yemeni women as war agents and contributors (Middle East Monitor, 2017). This contrasts with the traditional view and narrative that women are "beautiful souls" as Sjoberg (2010, p. 64) described. The ongoing crisis in the country has undermined the religious values and tribal traditions that hindered women's development and empowerment (Al-Iryani, 1998). As the crisis continues, it has provided new opportunities for women to take direct involvement and defend their country. Afshar (2003, pp. 2–3) points out the changes brought by war "create a sense of equality and erase gender differences." Examining the adaptability of customary law to changing circumstances, Adra (2016, pp. 316–317) argues that the rural population in Yemen is characterized by its ability to adapt to the new circumstances of war and crisis. Additionally, the deaths of fathers and husbands in the war has forced women to break out of traditional gender roles and become the breadwinners (Alkhayat and Rayes, 2016). Yemen's history is illustrative of powerful queens and strong-willed women leaders (Adra, 2016, p. 317).

In fact, women's subordination resulted from foreign-imposed fundamentalist ideologies that have found their way into rural society through teachers and the school curriculum designed by Islamists with strong ties to the Gulf states, particularly Saudi Arabia (Strzelecka, 2013, para 12). The Islamist movements in Yemen, namely those adopting Wahhabism, the Muslim Brotherhood, and modern Salafism are not indigenous to Yemen. As Adra (2016, p. 326) researched rural areas of Yemen in the early 1970s, she found that women outside their homes barely covered themselves below the knee in some rural areas. The rural population of Yemen has valued women's mobility and self-confidence, which is now considered as something of the past (Adra 2016, p. 327). Makhlouf (2016, pp. 50–55) also shares this view in her research on the impact of modernization in northern Yemen. Urban Yemeni women complain that women are no longer as visible in public spaces as they were twenty years ago (Adra, 2016, p. 327).

Conclusion

Despite the stated equality between men and women in the Islamic tradition as well as in the Yemeni constitution, urbanization and Islamization have created a starkly segregated society in which women play minor roles beyond their households. The 2011 revolution brought back renewed hopes for greater inclusion of women in public affairs, especially as women had played key leading roles in the events of 2011. The current war has changed the dynamics of women's engagement in public matters. The death of primary providers of families has compelled women to enter traditionally male areas. Also, the Houthis have utilized women for both suppressing dissenting women's voices as well as helping in the war effort through donation collection, recruitment of soldiers, food logistics, and in policing work. The political participation and civic engagement of Yemeni women has recently diminished as a result of the conflict and the use of women (Al-Zainabiyat) to crack down on female activists.

Overall, Yemeni women have always been powerful members of their society. Throughout history, women have participated in labour and policing work. In the last two decades, the state gave women more opportunities to participate in all aspects of public life, and to have an impact on all spheres of development and peacebuilding. In fact, the former regime enlisted thousands of women in the army and security apparatus. The female combatants were not used by the regime during the three decades to crack down on protests or activism. Rather, the regime has maintained the social norms and kept women's freedom of choice intact. What changed recently is that the Houthis have used women, particularly those loyal to Hashemite families, to infringe on the social norms and respectable status of women by using them to commit grave human rights violations and suppression of activism and freedom.

References

Abohajeb, A. (2020). *Personal Communication with Women's Activists, Social Figures, and Academics*, Sanaa.

Adra, N. (2010). "Tribal Mediation in Yemen and its Implications to Development." *AAS Working Papers in Social Anthropology* 19: 1–19. http://www.najwaadra.net/tribalmediation.pdf.

———— (2016). "Tribal Mediation and Empowered Women: Potential Contributions of Heritage to National Development in Yemen." *International Journal of Islamic Architecture* 5, no. 2: 301–337.

Addin, M. S. (2016). *Yemen's Houthis and Former President Saleh: An Alliance of Animosity*. Paris: Policy Alternative, Arab Reform Initiative, 1–2.

Afshar, H. (2003). "Women and Wars: Some Trajectories Towards a Feminist Peace." *Development in Practice* 13, no. 2–3: 178–188.

Al Arabiya Network (2017a). "Learn about 'Al-Zinbiyat': Houthi Secret Weapon in Yemen," *Al Arabiya Network*, December 10. http://ara.tv/6vk4n.

Al-Arabiya Network (2017b). "Who are the 'Descendants of Zainab', the Houthis' all-female brigade?" *Al-Arabiya Network*. December 11. http://Ara.tv/2gqcm.

Al-Iryani, A. (1998). "Yemen: The Role of the State in a Traditional Society." *Al-Bab*. Accessed January 6, 2018. http://al-bab.com/yemen-role-state-traditional-society.

Aljroui, N. (2017). "Interview of Noura Aljroui: GPC Female Member and Activist." *You tube video*, 10:40. Posted by "Sarou Hammir." December 23, 2017. https://www.youtube.com/watch?v=IJebPQXWjkc.

Alkhayat, M. and Rayes, Y. (2016). "Yemeni Women Break Taboos to Become Family Breadwinners." *Middle East Eye*. August 09, 2016. http://www.middleeasteye.net/in-depth/features/hfr-yemen-women-break-taboo-support-family-2069553815.

Al-Nu'man, M. (2018). "About the Hashemites in Yemen." *Okaz News Press*. January 6, 2018. http://www.okaz.com.sa/article/1603783/.

Al-Sakkaf, N. (2012). Yemen's Women and the Quest for Change. In *Political Participation after the Arab Revolution*.

Al-Salahi, J. (2018). "Street Shia." *You Tube video*, 3: 04. Posted by "Jalal Al - Salahi Videos." January 8, 2018. https://www.youtube.com/watch?v=JYYEY4vPhc0.

Alwazir, A. (2016). "Yemen's Enduring Resistance: Youth between Politics and Informal Mobilization." *Mediterranean Politics* 21, no. 1: 170–191.

Baghdad Post. (2017). "Houthis Intensify Female Recruitment, Violate Women's Rights in Yemen." *Baghdad Post*. December 11, 2017. http://s.thebaghdadpost.com/en/20800.

Beck, M. and Hüser, S. (2012). "Political Change in the Middle East: An Attempt to Analyze the 'Arab Spring'." GIGA Working Paper 203.

Buringa, J. (1988). *Yemeni Women in Transition: How Development Cooperation Could Fit In*. The Hague, Netherlands: Ministry of Foreign Affairs.

Finn, T. (2015). "Yemen's Women Revolutionaries." *The Dissent Magazine*. Accessed January 9, 2018. https://www.dissentmagazine.org/article/yemen-women-revolutionaries-arab-spring-2011-tawakkol-karman.

Heinze, M. (2017). "Women Nowadays Do Anything." *Safer World*. Accessed December 24, 2017. https://www.academia.edu/33605246/Women_Nowadays_Do_Anything_Women_s_Role_in_Conflict_Peace_and_Security_in_Yemen.

Hennessey, K. (2015). "Staging the Revolution: The Drama of Yemen's Arab Spring." *Arabian Humanities, International Journal of Archaeology and Social Sciences in the Arabian Peninsula* 4, http://journals.openedition.org/cy/2848.

Jubran, J. (2011). "Tribal Norms are a last Resort for Yemeni Women." *Al-akhbar*. Accessed January 5, 2018, http://www.al-akhbar.com/node/24554.

Makhlouf, C. (2016). *Changing Veils: Women and Modernisation in North Yemen*. New York: Routledge.

Middle East Monitor (2017). "Yemen Houthi Women Hold a Parade in Sana'a." *The Middle East Monitor*. January 19. https://www.middleeastmonitor.com/20170119-yemen-houthi-women-hold-a-parade-in-sanaa/.

National Democratic Institute (NDI) (2003). "Parliamentary Elections Yemen: Women's Participation." *National Democratic Institute*. Accessed January 7, 2018. https://www.ndi.org/sites/default/files/Parl%20Elections%20Yemen%20part4.pdf.

Palik, J. (2017). "Dancing on the heads of snakes": The emergence of the Houthi movement and the role of securitizing subjectivity in Yemen's civil war." *Corvinus Journal of International Affairs* 2, no. 2–3: 42–56.

Sjoberg, L. (2010) "Women Fighters and the 'Beautiful Soul' Narrative." *International Review of the Red Cross* 92, no. 877: 53–68.

Snyder, S. (2017). "Yemen's Capital is Under Lockdown: Hear a First-Person Account." *Public Radio International*. Accessed December 22, 2017, https://

www.pri.org/stories/2017-12-08/listen-harrowing-account-yemen-s-post -assassination-lockdown.

Strzelecka, E. (2013). "Gender and Islam in Development Policy and Practice in Yemen." *Arabian Humanities, International Journal of Archaeology and Social Sciences in the Arabian Peninsula* 1. http://journals.openedition.org/cy/2062.

Taibah, N. J. and MacDonald, M. R. (2015). *Folktales from the Arabian Peninsula: Tales of Bahrain, Kuwait, Oman, Qatar, Saudi Arabia, The United Arab Emirates, and Yemen: Tales of Bahrain, Kuwait, Oman, Qatar, Saudi Arabia, The United Arab Emirates, and Yemen.* Santa Barbara, CA: Libraries Unlimited, ABC-CLIO.

The Jerusalem Post (2015). "Armed Houthi Women Threaten War against U.S, SAUDI ARABIA, ISRAEL," *The Jerusalem Post*, March 29, 2015, http://www .jpost.com/Middle-East/Watch-Armed-Houthi-woman-threaten-war-against-US -Saudi-Arabia-Israel-395487.

TOBE Foundation for Rights & Freedoms (2017). "Status of Women during Conflict in Yemen." *TOBE Foundation for Rights & Freedoms*. Accessed January 7, 2018. http://www.tobeonline.org/NDetails.aspx?contid=63.

UNDP (2017). "Everyday Heroes: Amidst conflict, Yemeni women find ways to lead." United Nations Development Programme. December 8. https://medium .com/@UNDP/yemeni-women-under-siege-find-ways-to-lead-3f60622d36a2.

United Nations Security Council (UNSC) (2020). "Final Report of the Panel of Experts on Yemen." *UNSC*. https://www.un.org/securitycouncil/sanctions/2140 /panel-of-experts/work-and-mandate/reports

Weir, S. (2007). *A Tribal Order: Politics and Law in the Mountains of Yemen.* Austin: University of Texas Press.

Zanelli, P. (2013). "In Focus n° 3: Sana'a and Rapid Urbanization in some Short Stories by Muḥammad alGharbī 'Amrān." *Arabian Humanities, International Journal of Archaeology and Social Sciences in the Arabian Peninsula* 2. http:// journals.openedition.org/cy/2611.

8 Youth engagement

From uprising to fragile political transition in Yemen

Elham Raweh

Introduction

In early 2011 the wave of uprisings in the so-called Arab Spring was initially led by the youth against dictatorship and repression, demanding a better life, and Yemen was no exception. The youth had led the demonstrations against the rule of Ali Abdullah Saleh demanding change that spanned almost the whole country, where the youth put forward their hopes and needs, demanding their fundamental human rights and freedoms (OHCHR, 2011). In March 2011, the Gulf Cooperation Council (GCC) initiative was launched by Saudi Arabia to prevent the escalation of violence in Yemen (Asseburg et al., 2018). Jamal Benomar was first appointed by the UN Secretary-General as Special Envoy for Yemen to reinforce with his good offices the efforts of the GCC in Yemen. By November 2011, taking into account that the youth were entirely excluded from the initiative, the former president Saleh agreed to hand over power to his deputy Abd Rabbu Mansour Hadi by signing the GCC initiative and then starting the implementation mechanism that led to the National Dialogue Conference (NDC) launching in 2013 in which women and youth were well represented with 30% and 20% quotas, respectively (Mancini and Vericat, 2016).

Yemen was the only country of the Arab Spring upheavals where the president stepped down by means of a structured, negotiated power-sharing agreement, that was also supported internationally with its transition process (Zyck, 2014). Even so, this transitional period faced several obstacles that unfortunately led to a devastating war. Conflict erupted in 2014 when the Al-Houthi movement (Ansar Allah) took over the capital, Sana'a, and was further escalated with the response launched by the Saudi-led coalition to restore president Hadi's government and secure Saudi Arabia's borders (Al-Rawhani, 2018). Since then, violence has continued to shatter the country with no agreement or peace accord seemingly happening any time soon. The latest was in December 2018, the Stockholm agreement (OSESGY, 2019), was for Al-Hodeida to cease military operations that are still stumbling with the constant absence of trust between the conflict parties and failed to de-escalate the conflict (Aldroubi, 2019). Despite the declaration made by the Saudi coalition in April 2020 to a ceasefire in a bid to control the COVID-19 pandemic, there were no major effects on land battles nor any air strikes (UN News, 2020). The UN attempted to bring the conflict parties to the negotiation table, yet youth were not officially represented, neither were women. Meanwhile, Yemen is facing the worst man-made humanitarian crisis in the world, leading to the collapse of the state and its infrastructure (OCHA-Yemen, 2020).

Since the youth uprising in 2011, the world has witnessed how young people can play an effective role in changing their lives as "today's generation of youth is the largest the world has ever known and they often form the majority of the population in countries affected by armed conflict" (UNSCR 2535, 2020, p. 1). With such a huge youthful structure, an estimated of three-quarters of Yemen's population is under the age of 30, according to the World Population Prospect of 2019 data booklet, youth form 60% of the Yemeni population (United Nations, 2019). Around 43% are under the age of 15 (UNFPA Yemen, 2016) and another 23.17% are youth between 15 and 24 years (Countrymeters, 2020), the majority of whom are unemployed – 24.04% in July 2020 – due to the limited availability of job opportunities and the deteriorated economic status (World Bank, 2020).

The United Nations Security Council unanimously adopted a historic resolution on youth, peace, and security, UNSCR 2250, announced on December 9, 2015 (UN, 2015). The resolution recognized youth contribution to conflict resolution and the peace process. Highlighting five key pillars for action: participation, partnership, prevention, protection and disengagement, and reintegration (UN, 2017). This was followed by the progress study recommendations and findings – the independent progress study on youth peace and security: "The Missing Peace" that was presented on March 2, 2018 – that demonstrated young people's positive role in sustaining peace and as a result of that, the second UNSCR 2419 was the second resolution adopted in 2018 (youth4peace, 2018a). The resolution urges the member states to consider the youth's views and to facilitate their equal participation in decision making (UN, 2018; youth-4peace, 2018b). On July 14, 2020, the UN Security Council adopted a new resolution, 2523, that recognizes young people's role in strengthening local communities' capacities during and in post-conflict situations (UN, 2020).

Youth

Youth could be defined as a term that indicates a period of time in a person's life and according to age "when a young person has not yet become an adult" (Merriam-Webster, 2020). The United Nations defines "youth" as those persons between the ages of 15 and 24 merely for statistical purposes (UN, 1985). However, UNSCR 2250 (2015) defines youth as "persons of the age of 18–29" while there might be variations in utilizing the term in other UN agencies and national contexts (UNSCR 2250, 2015, p. 1). The Amman Youth Declaration, (2015) defines:

> We, young people, are highly engaged in transforming conflict, countering violence, and building peace. Yet, our efforts remain largely invisible.

In the Constitutional Guidelines on Youth in Yemen, as per National Dialogue Conference Outcomes Document, it stated the required empowerment shall be given to youth under 40 years old with at least 20% representation in the governing bodies of political parties (Lahrach, 2014, p. 8). Secondly, the term "youth" can be defined according to different life stages on the "psychological perspective of the transitional phase of youthhood" (Anderson, 2019, p. 17) and that could be "personal experiences, social, cultural, biological (i.e., puberty) or psychological (i.e., when the youth adopt adult responsibilities due to changes brought about by conflict)" (Pratley, 2011, p. 26).

However, conceiving "youth" merely as an age category has been criticized widely as it separates the complex issues related to youth (Sukkar, 2018). Youth are not a homogeneous group, it is crucial to consider the diversity within each category such as "young women, young men, young victims, former young combatants, etc." (Quintilla, 2016). However, considering youth as a social construct also faced a critique of "what is not; youths are not fully dependent, neither are they fully independent, socially responsible adults" (De Waal and Argenti, 2002; Pratley, 2011). Pratley (2011), who outlined three constructions and how these differences of viewing youth can affect the responses in policymaking. First, youth as "victims" who are vulnerable and in need of protection and to be "cared for rather than active community members" (Pratley, 2011; Eyber and Ager, 2004, p. 189). Second, youth as troublemakers that presents youth-in-conflict in three forms as follows:

a) Perpetrators who are involved in hostilities or when their needs and aspirations are not fulfilled by their communities or government. Youth are seen as a destabilizing force because "when young people are uprooted, jobless, intolerant, alienated, and have few opportunities for positive engagement, they represent a ready pool of recruits for groups seeking to mobilize violence" (Pratley, 2011; USAID, 2010, p. 3).

b) Youth as triggers-of-conflict: when youth raise the security threats demanding change and more opportunities as a result of resource scarcities due to a "youth-bulge" which is defined as "extraordinarily large youth cohorts relative to the adult population" because youth-as-triggers are forced to compete for limited educational and employment opportunities where there is no armed conflict (Pratley, 2011; Urdal, 2004, p. 7). This construction was used as an explanation by several scholars – including in Yemen – for the political violence that occurred during the so-called Arab Spring when youth were leading the uprising. (Anderson, 2019; LaGraffe, 2012; Nordas and Davenport, 2013). This youth-as-trigger construction differs from the youth-as-perpetrator construction as it is typically situated outside armed conflict (Pratley, 2011).

c) Spoilers to peace processes: when elite youth who disrupt the peace process feel there are not enough incentives, such as political or economic gains, in order to give up violence (Pratley, 2011).

Pratley (2011, p. 45) defines youth-as-peacebuilders as "agents who contribute positively during and after periods of conflict."

Youth and agenda for peace

The agenda for youth, peace, and security (YPS) first recognized youth contributions in bringing about peace and the active role in conflict resolution by adopting its first resolution, 2250 (2015), and contains five key elements: prevention, protection, participation, disengagement, and reintegration of youth. The resolution utilized the term "meaningful inclusion" and "meaningful participation" interchangeably that can be related and emanated from the "women, peace, and security agenda, and its supporting resolution, UNSCR 1325, on peace and security adopted in 2000." It is noted in the report of Women's Meaningful Participation in Peace Negotiation and the Implementation of Peace Agreements (UN Women, 2018) that "meaningful" is used when expressing a "positive and aspirational outlook on the progress of a more inclusive decision-making" (Anderson, 2019).

The UNSCR 2250 is considered to be a change in this dichotomy around the possibility of youth radicalization, uneducated youth, weak young women, unemployed youth, and criminalization of young people (Anderson, 2019; Özerdem and Podder, 2015). However, some scholars criticized the agenda for youth peace and security as an attempt to "securitize youth" according to Sukarieh and Tannock (2017). The global securitization of youth, which they argue UNSCR 2250 is a result of securitization of development. They also criticized the use of "youth bulge" in the resolution (Sukarieh and Tannock, 2017). The UNSCR (2250, 2015) requested the Secretary-General "to carry out a progress study on the youth's positive contribution to peace processes and conflict resolution, in order to recommend effective responses at local, national, regional and international levels." The independent progress study on youth peace and security; the "Missing Peace" was carried out as independent research led by Graeme Simpson and an Advisory Group of Experts, they were all appointed by the Secretary-General of the United Nations (UN, 2018).

Youth peacebuilders or Peace-spoilers?

The war that is being fought throughout the world today is being fought by youth. The peace that will be fought for throughout the world tomorrow must also be fought by youth.

(Glaser, 1944, p. 172)

Since the escalation of conflict in 2015, the Office of the Special Envoy of the Secretary-General for Yemen (OSESGY) has been working with stakeholders on TrackI (official politicians) less often than with TrackII and other stakeholders. However, the Yemeni youth are still excluded, with no formal representation in the political negotiation, despite the fact that UNSCR 2419 (2018) "calls for an increasing role of youth in negotiation and implementing the peace agreement" (UNSCR 2419, 2018). UNSCR 2523 (2020) in its para. 20 also requested:

The Secretary-General and his Special Envoys to include the views of youth in relevant discussions pertinent to the maintenance of peace and security, peacebuilding and sustaining peace, and to facilitate the full, effective and meaningful participation of youth at all decision-making levels, paying particular attention to the inclusion of young women and without distinction or discrimination of any kind.

(UNSCR 2535, 2020, p. 5)

On the other hand, the number of Yemeni youth who are aware of the UNSCRs are barely countable, according to a random study on a group of youth working in the field of peacebuilding only 25% know about UNSCR 2250, and only 9 out of 100 youth in Aden Governorate does (Alsakkaf, 2021a). Before 2011, Yemeni youth were active socially on a small scale in their local communities such as neighbourhoods or within youth union activity in schools and colleges. According to Maged Al-Kholidy, head of Youth Without Borders Organization for Development, "Youth unions were active, and despite the factional control over them during that period, youth's role was effective at the district and governorate level" (Al-Kholidy, 2020). During the 2011 upheavals, the youth were leading the peaceful demonstrations demanding change for a better life including the political and economic situations. The youth were seen as agents of democratic change, and as active political agents, which was why political actors "rushed to use them as leverage in the political arenas" (Al-Kholidy et al., 2020, p. 3).

The peaceful youth movement turned to an elite power struggle among the major established political parties who ousted them from the GCC initiative and co-opted the movement (Thiel, 2012). Yemeni youth felt like it was a "complete betrayal" (Lackner, 2016, p. 38). It is worth noting that, during the so-called Arab Spring uprising, the UN was quite slow to get involved in places like Egypt and Syria, unlike in Yemen (Mancini and Vericat, 2016). In April 2011, Jamal Benomar was appointed as a special adviser on Yemen by the UN Secretary-General, just two months following the uprisings that emerged in the country, to support the efforts of the GCC in Yemen with his good offices. As the UN Special Envoy to Yemen, Benomar acted very quickly, arrived in the country, and started to work with all layers of the Yemeni key actors, youth in particular, despite the fact that he had no mandate to work from the Security Council (SC) or General Assembly (Mancini and Vericat, 2016). This unique action "established a crucial space for dialogue" and helped to open spaces for national dialogue and encourage planning for a better future for Yemen apart from chaos (Zyck, 2014).

Benomar then refined the Implementation Mechanism of the GCC Initiative in such a way that it received broad buy-in nationally. He was successfully leading the transition plan, the National Dialogue Conference (NDC) in particular, where he ensured inclusion for women and youth and other marginalized segments to be presented. The NDC's 565 participants consisted of 30% women and 20% youth (Zyck, 2014) as a result of Benomar's push for inclusivity and reaching out to a wide range of stakeholders from Yemeni society (Mancini and Vericat, 2016). It set a great example for inclusion in its basic forms "Benomar reached out beyond the traditional power holders and warring parties to ordinary people demonstrating in the squares asking for change" (Mancini and Vericat, 2016, p. 15). For many youths, their participation in the NDC was breaking through normalization of the existing political sphere. "Youth presence in the NDC for the first time, institutionalized youth participation in the political process ever since," said Farea Aluslimi the head of the Sana'a Centre for Strategic Studies (Al-muslimi, 2020).

Even though the result of these attempts was to bring about a deep "paradigm shift" (Kuhn, 1962), the process as a whole remained centred on elites (Sukarieh and Tannock, 2017, p. 15). Youth participation in the NDC could be seen as an "inside room" and youth were present, but not "well-represented." Another young female from Aden Governorate said, "we had the seat at the table, yet our voices were unheard". That also could be seen in the outcomes of the NDC that did not deal with youth issues, nor were the points suggested by youth attending. Shatha Al-Harazi, a youth representative in the NDC explained during the First International Symposium on Youth Participation in Peace Processes, "even though we had a seat at the table, we didn't feel as though we were meaningfully involved" (YPPP, 2019). During the symposium, Shatha also talked about the selection process of the applicants to the NDC, which was frustrating to many youth applicants as the process went by key pre-selected representatives only (YPPP, 2019).

After 2011, with the collapse of the political transition in 2014, the opportunities for Yemeni youth abounded, although their political involvement was not meaningful, "NGOs are fighting over funding in the name of youth in a competition that is for greater influence, yet, it becomes negative, and youth participation is a merely 'check box' for donors," said a young male activist (*Interview No.14, Anonymous*, 2020). On the other hand, the "Youth participation in the political process is no longer a priority for youth, unlike what happened during 2011, their priorities are finding a living, income, education, etc.," said Yazeed Al-Jeddawy, the regional representative of the United Network of Young (UNOY) "not to mention that no one entity that is agreed among youth to represent them," continued Yazeed (Al-Jeddawy, 2020). Another young female from Taiz said, "we are afraid of political participation, we lost trust in everyone" (*Interview No.9, anonymous*, 2020). In addition, Yemeni politicians no longer include youth in the peace talks process or international opportunities as they dwindled (Transfeld, 2019). Olla Alsakkaf a Yemeni youth activist said:

> Young people constitute the popular base for the political parties, but they are tools for their agendas, and the decision-making lies with the adults who fear losing their personal interests if they got more youth involved.
>
> (Alsakkaf, 2021)

The severe deterioration in the current situation in Yemen affected youth in many ways; from the lack of security to restrictions on movement, the economic collapse that resulted in many job losses, restrictions on freedoms, and detainment of youth activists, all that affected youth activism and their volunteerism (al-Kholidy et al., 2020). With a major population of youth who live in urban areas which constitute more than 63% of the Yemeni population (WorldBank, 2019), youth are being attracted to battles, used as the fuel for armed hostilities, and have been involved in the devastating conflict since late 2014. "Youth have been used by belligerents as an agent of war but not as agent for peace nor as peacebuilders," said Omar Baras, Head of Wa3i Foundation, (Baras, 2020). On the front lines of those deadly hostilities only youth are paying the cost with their lives (Alsakkaf, 2021). As a result, Yemeni youth are driven to leave the country or run for their lives, "I had to escape the country to save my life by applying for a protection request in a foreign country and for a living," said a young man from Ibb Governorate (*Interview No.4, anonymous*, 2020). And for those who are inside remain with limited opportunities

> our youth is a wasted energy because we don't have places that help us be more active, specifically after war shut down, we don't find much to do in our free time with limited financial income, hence chewing Qat is our best and last resort to spend our time with other friends better than going for worse things

said a 28-year-old male from Sana'a Governorate (*Interview No.3, anonymous*, 2020).

Maher Othman, a Yemeni public policy analyst stated, "In a country that is characterized by having a young society, this group is expected to play a pivotal role in its development. Unfortunately, the policies towards youth over the past decades are considered a major reason for what the youth have lost till today" (Othman, 2021). Despite all that, the Yemeni youth are still active, especially at the local level. Yemeni youth are still convinced of their pivotal role in community civic engagement (Alsakkaf, 2021). "The politicians stole our dreams, so I wanted to carry on our dreams in a more structured and institutionalized way" quoted young activists (Saferworld, 2019).

As the conflict perpetuates and the humanitarian crisis worsens, youth are among the first responders to their community needs, they even led local negotiations to solve the disputes over livelihoods, such as water and gas pumps (Saferworld, 2019). Youth are very active at the community level, "Youth not only helped with humanitarian assistance distributions, but they were also active during the COVID-19 rapid response" said Olla Alsakkaf, she also added, "Youth-led initiatives helped in solving livelihood issues and water conflict in Taiz Governorate" (Alsakkaf, 2021).

Another group of youth in Abyan Governorate solved a conflict between two neighbourhoods in Mudiah district over electricity, by initiating a campaign to maintain the public electricity station and restore the electricity for the two neighbourhoods' houses by their voluntary efforts and continuous maintenance. This has encouraged another two neighbouring in Mudiah district in Abyan to imitate the experience and restore their public electricity and solve their neighbourhoods' conflict over electricity and convergence of the views of the disputants, according to Bahia Al-Sakkaf the executive manager of Alf BA Foundation (Al-Sakkaf, 2020). These initiatives and endeavours that that youth are doing on a daily basis, indeed, support the chapter's argument that youth can be an agent for peace locally through their connection and activities with their local communities.

Most recently, there are more attempts to get youths engaged with the political process with more projects and new youth platforms to get them involved (Al-aghbari, 2020). "The envoy's office did not pay much attention until December last year" (Baras, 2020). With this slowly momentum youth are sceptical "Although the political process is stalled yet, youth should be part of it, their aspirations and issues should be within the agreement to come and part of the solution" (*Interview No.14, anonymous*, 2020). "We as youth should advocate for common issues to be addressed in the negotiations irrespective of who is on the table" (Al-muslimi, 2020). "Inclusion is not a 'check box' for donors, we should stand against the mere presenting and defend the genuine engagement of youth" (*Interview No.14, anonymous*, 2020).

"Youth work is random and unorganized, but if it is organized into one channel, its impact will be stronger," said Nebras Anam a Yemeni researcher (Anam, 2020). Youth need to be prepared for the next level by building their capacity and preparing them for the next stage of the process.

Conclusion

After 2011, Yemeni youths made their voices heard and participated effectively. With the transitional process failing they were abandoned and used to fuel the conflict. However, most of them remain active and help their communities during the worsening humanitarian situation and COVID-19 pandemic. It is now a critical time to include youth and enforce change within the political process that brings about peace for Yemen. As the conflict perpetuates and the humanitarian crisis worsens, youth are among the first responders to their community needs, they even led local negotiations to solve the disputes over livelihoods such as water and gas pumps. They even mediate with the de facto authorities to open blocked roads for people to move and transfer aid supplies (Saferworld, 2019). These initiatives and endeavours that youth are doing on a daily basis, indeed, support the chapter's argument that is: youth can be an agent for peace locally through their connection and activities with their local communities and thus, youth participation in peace processes can be availed.

The chapter concludes that the UNSCRs and the YPSA are in their first step to bring youth to the centre and include them in the peace process, yet more efforts are still required. There are surely more success stories and lessons to be learned and found in more research studies. These can tell about the work done by youth and other local actors and their capabilities of forming a bottom-up peace in Yemen, or if not yet ready to do so, and may need further support, capacity building, and effective participation in order to reflect on the bigger conflict and influence the TrackI outcomes. Youths are tomorrows' leaders and the implementers of those peace agreements, reconstruction, and development plans; thus, it is essential to bring them to the centre and include them during the process.

References

Al-aghbari, O. (2020, September 15). *Interview No. 7* [In person/over Zoom].

Aldroubi, M. (2019, July 16). Yemen's peace process advances but trust remains an obstacle, experts say. *The National*. https://www.thenational.ae/world/mena/yemen-s-peace-process-advances-but-trust-remains-an-obstacle-experts-say-1.887006.

Al-Jeddawy, Y. (2020, August 27). *Interview No. 5* [In person/over Zoom].

Al-Kholidy, M. (2020, July). *Interview No. 2* [In person/over Zoom].

Al-Kholidy, M., al-Jeddaw, Y., and Nevens, K. (2020). The role of youth in peacebuilding in Yemen. *CARPO Briefs*. https://carpo-bonn.org/wp-content/uploads/2020/04/carpo_brief_17_27-04-20_EN.pdf.

Al-muslimi, F. (2020, September 5). *Interview No. 6* [In person].

Al-Najjar, M. (2010). Legislation and policies related to youth empowerment in a working paper submitted to the regional conference for youth empowerment in Yemen – Sana'a. *Felix News*. http://www.felixnews.com/news-5052.html.

Al-Rawhani, O. (2018). *Yemen's State (Re)building: A Tale of Too Many Obstacles | ISPI*. ISPI (Istituto per Gli Studi Di Politica Internazionale). https://www.ispionline.it/it/pubblicazione/yemens-state-rebuilding-tale-too-many-obstacles-19924.

Al-Sakkaf, B. (2020, November 30). *Interview No. 12* [In person/over Zoom].

Alsakkaf, O. (2021a). The impact of the YPS agenda on Yemeni youth (YOUTH LEADERSHIP OF UNSCR 2250) [case study]. *UNOY Peacebuilders*. https://unoy.org/en/resources/.

Alsakkaf, O. (2021b, January 22). *Interview No. 11* [In person].

Anam, N. (2020, July). *Interview No. 1* [In person/over Zoom].

Anderson, I. E. (2019). *Youth, Peace and Security A qualitative analysis of UNSCR 2250 and the international response to a new security agenda*. University of Oslo. http://www.duo.uio.no/.

Asseburg, M., Lacher, W., and Transfeld, M. (2018). *Mission Impossible? UN Mediation in Libya, Syria and Yemen*. 35. Stiftung Wissenschaft und Politik German Institute for International and Security Affairs. SWP Research Paper 8.

94 *Elham Raweh*

Baras, O. (2020, September 6). *Interview No. 10* [In person/over Zoom].

Countrymeters (2020). Yemen population (2020) live. *Countrymeters.* https://countrymeters.info/en/Yemen.

De Waal, A. and Argenti, N. (2002). *Young Africa: Realising the Rights of Children and Youth.* Africa World Press. http://books.google.com/books?id =xmSTAAAAIAAJ.

Eyber, C. and Ager, A. (2004). Researching young people's experiences of war: Participatory methods and the trauma discourse in Angola. *Children and Youth on the Front Line: Ethnography, Armed Conflict and Displacement, 14,* 189–208.

Glaser, A. B. (1944). Youth must lead fight for peace. *World Affairs, 107*(3), 172–177.

Interview No.3, anonymous (2020, August). [In person].

Interview No.4, anonymous (2020, August). [In person/over Zoom].

Interview No.9, anonymous (2020, September 10). [In person].

Interview No.14, anonymous (2020, September 5). [In person/over Zoom].

Kuhn, T. S. (1962). *The Structure of Scientific Revolutions.* Chicago: The University of Chicago Press.

Lackner, H. (2016). *Yemen's "Peaceful" Transition from Autocracy: Could It Have Succeeded?* Stockholm, Sweden: International Institute for Democracy and Electoral Assistance (International IDEA).

LaGraffe, D. (2012). The youth bulge in Egypt: an intersection of demographics, security, and the Arab spring. *Journal of Strategic Security, 5*(2). http://dx.doi.org/10.5038/1944-0472.5.2.4.

Lahrach, S. (2014). Constitutional guidelines on youth in Yemen: as per NDC outcomes document. *Women and Youth Forum - Office of the Special Advisor to the Secretary - General on Yemen.* https://osesgy.unmissions.org/sites/default/files/4-youth_constituional_guidlines_en.pdf.

Mancini, F. and Vericat, J. (2016). Lost in transition: UN mediation in Libya, Syria, and Yemen. *SSRN Electronic Journal,* 1–18. https://doi.org/10.2139/ssrn.2883306.

Merriam-Webster (2020). Youth: definition for English-language learners from Merriam-Webster's learner's dictionary. https://www.learnersdictionary.com/definition/youths.

Nordas, R. and Davenport, C. (2013). Fight the youth: youth bulges and state repression. *American Journal of Political Science, 57*(4), 926–940. JSTOR. https://doi.org/10.1111/ajps.12025.

OCHA-Yemen (2020). *Yemen Humanitarian Update Issue 6* (June 2020) (https://reliefweb.int/report/yemen/yemen-humanitarian-update-issue-6-june-2020-enar; p. 8). ReliefWeb. http://shorturl.at/aipvC.

OHCHR (2011, December 8). OHCHR | The youth of Yemen in the Arab spring. https://www.ohchr.org/EN/NewsEvents/Pages/TheYouthOfYemenInTheArabSpring.aspx.

OSESGY (2019). A year after the Stockholm agreement: where are we now? *OSESGY.* https://osesgy.unmissions.org/year-after-stockholm-agreement-where-are-we-now.

Othman, M. (2021, January 22). *Interview No. 13* [In person/over Zoom].

Özerdem, A. and Podder, S. (2015). *Youth in Conflict and Peacebuilding.* New York: Palgrave Macmillan. https://link.springer.com/book/10.1057/9781137314536.

Pratley, E. M. L. (2011). *'Youth'- victim, troublemaker or peacebuilder Constructions of youth-in-conflict in United Nations and World Bank youth policies.* Victoria University of Wellington.

Quintilla, R. O. (2016). UN Security Council Resolution 2250: Youth, Peace and Security (Policy Paper). International Catalan Institute for Peace (ICIP), *14*, 6.

Saferworld (2019). *The situation needs us to be active" Youth contributions to peacebuilding in Yemen.* Saferworld. https://www.saferworld.org.uk/resources/ publications/1241-athe-situation-needs-us-to-be-activea-youth-contributions-to -peacebuilding-in-yemen.

Sukarieh, M. and Tannock, S. (2017). The global securitisation of youth. *Third World Quarterly*, *39*(5), 854–870.

Sukkar, B. (2018). "Youth" of Syria: an antithesis to an authoritarian system of power. In A. S. Okyay and L. Kamel (Eds), *Realizing Youth Potential in the Mediterranean Unlocking Opportunities, Overcoming Challenges* (pp. 21–34). Edizioni Nuova Cultura For Istituto Affari Internazionali (IAI). http://www.iai.it /sites/default/files/iairs_2.pdf.

Thiel, T. (2012). *After the Arab Spring: Power Shift in the Middle East?: Yemen's Arab Spring: From Youth Revolution to Fragile Political Transition* (Monograph No. SR011; Issue SR011). LSE IDEAS, London School of Economics and Political Science. http://www2.lse.ac.uk/IDEAS/Home.aspx.

Transfeld, M. (2019). *Youth Activism in the Yemeni Civil War.* Yemen Polling Center. https://www.yemenpolling.org/2664-2/.

UN (2015, December 9). *Security Council, Unanimously Adopting Resolution 2250 (2015), Urges Member States to Increase Representation of Youth in Decision-Making at All Levels | Meetings Coverage and Press Releases.* Meetings Coverage and Press Releases. https://www.un.org/press/en/2015/sc12149.doc .htm.

UN (2018). *The Missing Peace: Independent Progress Study on Youth, Peace and Security | PEACEBUILDING.* PEACEBUILDING. https://www.un.org/ peacebuilding/news/missing-peace-independent-progress-study-youth-peace -and-security.

UN (2020, July 14). *Security Council Underlines Vital Role of Youth in Building Peace, Unanimously Adopting Resolution 2535 (2020) | Meetings Coverage and Press Releases.* https://www.un.org/press/en/2020/sc14251.doc.htm.

UNFPA Yemen (2016, March 29). *About Yemen.* UNFPA Yemen. https://yemen .unfpa.org/en/about-yemen.

United Nations (1985). *Youth.* United Nations. https://www.un.org/en/sections/ issues-depth/youth-0/.

United Nations, D. of E. and S. A., Population Division (2019). *World Population Prospects 2019: Data Booklet* ((ST/ESA/SER.A/424)). https://www.un-ilibrary .org/population-and-demography/world-population-prospects-2019-data -booklet_3e9d869f-en.

UN Inter-Agency Network on Youth Development. (2017, July 11). *Resources on Youth, Peace and Security | United Nations For Youth*. United Nations Youth. https://www.un.org/development/desa/youth/international-youth-day-2017/resources-on-youth-peace-and-security.html.

UN News (2020, April 9). *COVID-19 in Yemen: Saudi coalition ceasefire declared in bid to contain coronavirus*. News. https://news.un.org/en/story/2020/04/1061422.

UNSCR 2250 (2015). *UNSCR 2250*. https://www.un.org/press/en/2015/sc12149.doc.htm.

UNSCR 2419 (2018). https://www.un.org/press/en/2018/sc13368.doc.htm.

UNSCR 2535 (2020, July 12). *UNSCR 2535*. https://undocs.org/pdf?symbol=en/S/RES/2535(2020).

UN Women (2018). *Women's Meaningful Participation in Negotiating Peace and the Implementation of Peace Agreements: Report of the Expert Group Meeting*. https://www.unwomen.org/en/digital-library/publications/2018/10/egm-report-womens-meaningful-participation-in-negotiating-peace.

Urdal, H. (2004). *The Devil in the Demographics: The Effect of Youth Bulges on Domestic Armed Conflict, 1950–2000* (No. 14; p. 31). Conflict Prevention and Reconstruction Unit, World Bank. https://www.prio.org/Publications/Publication/?x=489.

USAID (2010). *Youth and Conflict. A Toolkit Intervention*. United States Agency for International Development. https://resourcecentre.savethechildren.net/library/youth-and-conflict-toolkit-intervention.

World Bank (2019, December). *Rural population (% of total population)—Yemen, Rep. | Data*. The World Bank Data Indicator. https://data.worldbank.org/indicator/SP.RUR.TOTL.ZS?locations=YE.

World Bank (2020, July 1). Yemen: Youth unemployment rate from 1999 to 2019 [Graph]. *In Statista*. Retrieved August 12, 2020. https://www.statista.com/statistics/813178/youth-unemployment-rate-in-yemen/.

youth4peace (2018a, March). *Progress Study on Youth, Peace and Security*. https://www.youth4peace.info/ProgressStudy.

youth4peace (2018b). *UNSCR 2419 | Youth4Peace Portal*. https://www.youth4peace.info/unscr2419.

YPPP (2019). *First International Symposium on Youth Participation in Peace Processes [Summary Report]*. https://www.un.org/youthenvoy/2019/02/first-international-symposium-on-youth-participation-in-peace-processes/.

Zyck, S. A. (2014). *Mediating Transition in Yemen: Achievements and Lessons*. New York: International Peace Institute, 20.

9 Youth in post-conflict reconstruction

The case of the Gaza Strip

Wadee Alarabeed

Introduction

Youth participation is seen as the active involvement of young people in their societies throughout all levels of political, social, and economic life, in a manner that enables them to achieve their aspirations, improve their standard of life, and influence decision-making circles (Checkoway and Gutierrez, 2008, p. 1). Those young people are considered as a vital component for development, social change, economic growth, and technological innovation (Campbell and Erbstein, 2012, p. 69). In conflict zones, there is a lack of youth participation in peacebuilding processes, reconciliation programmes, and post-conflict reconstruction initiatives, leading to a state of desperation among youth and the desire to leave their societies, as is the case in the Gaza Strip (Interpeace and United Nations, 2017, p. 5).

Following the Israeli military invasion against Gaza in 2014, the reconstruction of Gaza catapulted to the international headlines when more than 50 states pledged to provide funds of US$5.082 billion for rebuilding the coastal enclave, in "an international conference [was] held in Cairo in October 2014" (Zureik, 2018, p. 4). After several months, the reconstruction process was started without paying attention to the role of youth, and they were excluded from the process entirely (Abumidain, 2020). Over the past decades, Palestinian youth have played a major role in their societies through the active involvement in peacebuilding initiatives at both national and international levels. However, this role was undermined because of several factors: the ongoing Israeli occupation and the Palestinian political rift between Hamas – the de facto government in Gaza – and the Fatah-led Palestinian Authority (PA) in the West Bank (Swart, 2019). These factors have severely contributed to reducing the possibility of engaging a youth component in the reconstruction efforts in the aftermath of the 2014 war against the Gaza Strip.

Modern trends in the post-conflict reconstruction literature assert widely on the participation of the local population and young people, considering it as an important pillar in the reconstruction efforts (Clarke et al., 2010, p. 82). Recent studies also conclude that "… the planning and implementation of reconstruction should take place at various levels and with attention to the key needs and priorities of the local population," as Barakat reminds us that "ultimately, reconstruction is the promotion of a mindset fostered through a process of community empowerment" (Barakat, 2005a, p. 13).

The crucial factor here is how we can motivate the engagement of young people in peace initiatives, including in post-war reconstruction operations.

Youth and post-war reconstruction initiatives

After World War II, the international community was shocked and exhausted. As a result of this massive war the Marshal Plan emerged with the purpose of rebuilding a war-shattered Europe. For advocates, the Marshall Plan embodied a model of post-war reconstruction programmes (Wilson, 1977, p. 6), but, nevertheless, critics look at it as an American policy to control the nations of Western Europe through aid and assistance programmes, in order to halt the Russian threat to the US and Western Europe (O'Brien, 2014).

Moreover, according to the World Bank, post-war reconstruction crystallized around "economic recovery and normalization" while the UN concentrated on the importance of the political approach (Barakat, 2005b, pp. 572–573). However, the highly contextual nature of post-war reconstruction necessitates that the definition is not considered from only one point of view. Further, the UN believes that reconstruction activities demand "extensive human, knowledge and financial investments" (Zyck, 2016, p. 1). Controversially, Barakat and Zyck (2009, pp. 1071–1072) strongly suggest that "the concept of post-conflict reconstruction should be conceptualized by its aims and objectives, namely, to reactivate economic and social development, and to create a peaceful environment that will prevent a relapse into violence." To achieve development and focus on post-conflict reconstruction's aims and objectives, youth participation cannot be ignored, and their role must be essential from the start of the process. As Siobhan McEvoy-Levy explains:

> Youth should be represented in political negotiations, peace processes, and in transitional justice and reconstruction efforts for at least four reasons, therefore: because they had roles in the conflicts and struggles that went before; because they have rights to participation; because they also have important knowledge and ideas to contribute; and because long-term, sustained peace requires intergenerational healing. But building capacity among elite decision-makers, as well as among

youth, will be crucial. The capacity to share power with young people needs to be built at the highest levels.

(McEvoy-Levy, 2014, para 24)

Thus, young people must be included in post-war reconstruction efforts in a way that guarantees them political, social, and economic participation. This applies to the young people in the Gaza Strip, who have lived in a conflict zone since 1967.

The Gaza Strip context

The Gaza Strip is exposed to a set of complex interconnected problems, which present many dilemmas at both the theoretical and practical level. In particular, the Palestinian context is largely unique due to certain factors related to the existing Israeli colonial structure, the absence of basic elements of the state, a highly sensitive political, economic, and social environment which are subjected to the direct exposure to global and regional changes, and the intense participation of external actors (Da'na, 2014, p. 117). According to the Israeli Legal Centre (Gisha, 2011, p. 5) "there are three parties who exert the most control over the lives of Gaza's residents – namely Israel, the Hamas regime, and the Palestinian authority." In June 2007, the political situation deteriorated and became more complicated with the eruption of the political rift between the two most powerful political forces on the Palestinian scene, Fateh and Hamas (Høigilt et al., 2013, p. 1). Since then, the Hamas government has taken control of the Gaza Strip, and the PA led by Fateh has become stable in the West Bank (Rahman, 2019, p. 2). With the Hamas movement's rise to power in 2007, Israel imposed an unprecedented land, sea, and air blockade on the whole territory, followed by three repeated wars in just ten years, destroying its stability. Considering the fact that Gaza is under Israeli occupation, polls agree on the negative impact of the Palestinian political conditions and the Palestinian–Israeli conflict on the Palestinian youth who feel disappointed by the politics, the peace process, and their leadership (Høigilt et al., 2013, p. 1).

Furthermore, since the beginning of the Israeli occupation of Palestine, youths have fully engaged in the resistance against the occupation, as well as in the establishment of political factions and civil society organizations, among many others, attempting to build the emerging Palestinian state (Interpeace and United Nations, 2017, p. 18). After the signing of the Oslo Accord between Israel and the Palestinian Liberation Organization (PLO), the Palestinian national movement retreated, and the role of the youth has reduced (Abu Rukba, 2020).

With the start of the brutal blockade imposed on the Gaza Strip by Israel, particularly in 2006, after Hamas captured the Israeli soldier, Gilad Shalit (Chomsky and Pappé, 2013, p. 121), the economic, political, social, and psychological conditions have collapsed in the Gaza Strip. The Palestinian Central Bureau of Statistics (PCBS) states in 2017 that

> The percentage of youth in the age group of (15-29) in Palestine comprises 30% of the total population, distributed by 36% in the age group of (15-19) years and 64% in the age group of (20-29) years old. Where the sex ratio among the youth is 104 males per 100 females, noting that the population estimates in Palestine in mid-2017 indicate that the total population approximately reached 4.95 million, of them 2 million in Gaza.

(PCBS, 2017)

Also, the percentage of unemployed young people aged 15–29 is 40% among the youth involved in the labour force. Unemployed individuals aged 20–24 were the most affected group – 44% compared to the 36% unemployment rate among individuals aged 25–29 (PCBS, 2017).

In addition, from 2004 on, Israel has launched 22 military campaigns against Gaza, including Operation Protective Edge (2014), Operation Pillar of Cloud (2012), and Operation Cast Lead (2008–2009) (Erakat, 2019, p. 179). After the horrible war inflicted on Gaza in the summer of 2014, an international conference was held in Cairo in October 2014 to raise funds for the reconstruction of the Gaza Strip. During this period, 50 countries pledged to allocate US$5.082 billion for the reconstruction, though to date reports show that half of the amount has not been fulfilled (Zureik, 2018, p. 5).

The impact of the 2014 war against Gaza resulted in a total of 18,000 housing units being destroyed in whole or part, 73 medical facilities and many ambulances were damaged, 31 educational facilities were totally damaged, among many others (UNITAR, 2014). The repeated eruption of violence in the Gaza strip since the end of 2014 war affected all aspects of life in Gaza, including the economy. The World Bank also recognizes the dire economic conditions of the Gaza Strip, and predicts that "the Palestinian economy is expected to slip into negative growth in 2020 and 2021" (The World Bank, 2019). This affirms the negative and destructive influence of consecutive wars, sieges, and restrictions imposed on the entrance of money, goods, and materials into Gaza. Nonetheless, the violence erupted again on March 30, 2018 – the so-called "Palestinian Land Day" – when thousands of Palestinians started non-violent demonstrations in the "Great March of Return" (GMR) demonstrations to demand the end of the Israeli blockade and the right of return for refugees (UNRWA, 2019, p. 6). These peaceful marches were held on the Gaza borders each Friday in which men, women and youth took part, were halted by the organizers – "the Commission of the Great March of Return" – at the end of December 2019 (MEMO, 2019).

The United Nations Office for the Coordination of Humanitarian Affairs (OCHA) has repeatedly warned about the excessive force being used by the Israeli soldiers against the civilian demonstrators (OCHA, 2020). The explosion of violence during the GMR has led to 214 demonstrators, including 44 children, who were killed in this context and more than 36,100, including approximately 8,800 children have been injured by live ammunition fired by Israeli forces (OCHA, 2020). Against this backdrop, the reconstruction efforts were still in progress, focussing only on material reconstruction. During the implementation of the reconstruction plan in the Gaza Strip, young people were not involved with the process (Abu Rukba, 2020). The reconstruction plan was implemented either under the Israeli surveillance through the Gaza Reconstruction Mechanism (GRM), its establishment was announced in September 2014, by the UN Middle East Envoy Robert Serry, "a UN-administered mechanism between the UN, the Government of Palestine, and the Government of Israel designed to monitor and regulate the flow of goods into and out of the Gaza Strip" (Barakat et al., 2018. p. 5).

The GRM was a choice between many in Gaza to implement reconstruction. In other words, besides the GRM, the reconstruction efforts were also implemented through other internal and external actors that support Hamas and Gaza. However, Hamas officials did not refuse the GRM, they dealt with it, and they also opened new channels to keep reconstruction efforts on track, and to keep money flows into Gaza with their total control. The Center for Strategic and International Studies, however, concurs that "the four essential pillars for reconstruction are security and public safety, justice and reconciliation, governance and participation, and economic and social progress" (Schwartz, 2010, p. 7). Considering these pillars, this chapter looks at youth participation as part of post-war reconstruction initiatives, which should be included from the start of such initiatives and at the highest levels.

Youth exclusion

Young people are the first ones to be exposed to danger and suffering during and after conflicts; they are the ones who always bear the negative consequences (UNDP, 2006. p. 5). The Institute of Community and Public Health at Birzeit University (2018) indicates that "the marginalization of young people in various areas (social, political, and economic) has negative effects on their well-being." In addition, the literature of post-war reconstruction confirms that one of the most effective ways for the success of reconstruction programmes is the existence of a full cooperation with the local community including consulting them, hearing their suggestions in a way that contributes to improving their living standards, economic situation, and stability (Gennip, 2005, p. 59). Furthermore, the Paris Declaration on Aid Effectiveness reaffirms several commitments to numerous guiding principles relevant to issues of ownership, harmonization, alignment, results, and mutual accountability (Chandy, 2011, pp. 1–3). In the Gaza Strip, there has been an absence of these principles in the GRM at all levels. While these issues are essential for community development and empowerment, it is important to underscore the bureaucratic and slow nature found in the GRM which excludes people at the level of decision-making, transforming them into aid recipients (Barakat et al., 2018, pp. 5–11).

Moreover, the ongoing violence during the GRM has put a severe strain on the entire health, economic, and social system in Gaza, including the services provided by donors to help the Gaza Strip. The unemployment rate increased and reached its highest rate (52.5%) in 2018 according to the PCBS. Also, the chances for youth participation in the reconstruction efforts were zero, in that all reconstruction projects were controlled from the start by either Israel through the GRM, the Hamas government, or the humanitarian organizations working in the field in Gaza, implementing the plans in their own way without any participation with the youth. A recent study conducted by Al-Aqsa University (2019) in the Gaza Strip, reveals that about half of Palestinians aged 18 and above have the desire to migrate, once they are able to do so (MAS, 2019, p. 2). The main cause was the economic situation, as reported by 83% of the surveyed sample (ibid.). Also, other studies show that Palestinians, especially the young, really feel paralyzed and desperate because they are being deprived of practising their civil and political rights, which leads them to travel abroad and try to seek other opportunities elsewhere (The New Arab, 2019).

The missing opportunity

Generally speaking, one can say that few experiences have paid real attention to youth participation in peacebuilding after conflict (Schwartz, 2010). Given the fact that youth employment is vital in post-war reconstruction programmes and a matter of great importance to both governments and the youth, some think that the reconstruction programmes should provide job opportunities for post-conflict communities. However, the view does not discuss the sustainability of these jobs and whether they are planned to be sustainable. In the Gaza context, the repeated wars have made the economic structure fragile, and unable to provide job opportunities for the labour force.

After the 2014 war, the reconstruction process came packed with promises to create many job opportunities for young people, along with other promises to rebuild the entire Gaza Strip. Data show that the unemployment rate in the Gaza strip was 31% in 2014; however, the percentage was drastically decreased to 10% by the end of 2016, the time that the reconstruction efforts was supposed to be completed (Barakat et al., 2018, p. 10).

As a result of the economic, social, and political pressures that youth were suffering from, several demonstrations erupted in the Gaza Strip demanding the Hamas government to uphold its responsibilities towards the youth and the population and provide them with job opportunities and a decent life (Holmes, 2019). In truth, these demonstrations did not call for the overthrow of the government. Rather, the youth went out to express their rejection of the dire social, political, and economic situation in Gaza. In a statement Lieberman, an Israeli official, sent a message to the Palestinians in the Gaza strip that, "You can choose between poverty and unemployment or work and making a livelihood, between hatred and bloodshed or coexistence and personal security" (Middle East Monitor, 2018). His statement was for the Palestinians to put pressure on the Hamas government, while most of the problems from which Gaza suffers are aligned to the Israeli siege and occupation.

So far, the reconstruction programme in Gaza has focussed on material support, particularly housing and shelter. It then explains how slow, bureaucratic, and top–down the implemented projects were (Barakat et al., 2018, p. 1). For this reason, the rate of unemployment decreased, but it is normal that the building of damaged houses, schools, and hospitals, etc., will provide temporary job opportunities but not sustainable ones. It is difficult to say that creating job opportunities in places where there is an ongoing conflict is easy considering the harsh conditions that exist and given the fact that donors and humanitarian organizations concentrate on the provision of basic needs such as food, shelter, and instant relief, etc. However, in the reconstruction period, it is recommended that the "employment creation" issue needs to be tackled from the first step and throughout "the process of return to normality" (Date-Bah, 2003, p. 60).

Depriving youths

The supposed reconstruction process of the Gaza strip has lacked young people's engagement in the decision-making circles, including donors, national, and international organizations. This level of exclusion makes young people frustrated and hopeless. Almasri (2020) explains that the exclusion of youth in the reconstruction programmes is mainly because of the absence of sustainable and long-term plans informing the actors' agenda, such as the Hamas government, the PA, Israel, and other organizations. A Study on Youth, Peace, and Security based on UN Resolution 2250 has agreed that the exclusion of youth in such initiatives emphasizes:

> Young people are absent from the processes of decision-making, community development and participation in building peace and achieving security. The consequences of this situation have been reflected on society, with youth being the most affected at all levels, losing numerous opportunities to develop and enhance their roles. They have become unemployed, with less education opportunities, less public participation, and little hope for a better future.
>
> (Interpeace and United Nations, 2017, p. 5)

The participation of young people in reconstruction activities and initiatives based on their vision and understanding of the community enables them to suggest appropriate solutions to improve the level of livelihood in society. However, in the Gaza context, young people have been through many challenges which have undermined their participation in such initiatives. For example, the need to get permission from the authorities to implement their initiatives and proposals, which are sometimes dismissed by the authorities (Interpeace and United Nations, 2017). While the youth perceive this as a constraint to their participation in society, the level of participation in the reconstruction efforts is not confined to the youth's own initiatives. Zeldin concurs that "youth participation in decision making often centers around the domains of skill and motivation related to instrumentality and teamwork" (Zeldin, 2004, p. 76).

In addition, Zeldin demonstrates many factors that motivated young people to engage in organizational governance. The most prominent domains were (1) the demonstration of respect for youth voice and competency by the organization, (2) the balance of power and relationships with adults, (3) a feeling of belonging and importance to the organization, and (4) the importance of youth contributing on their own terms (Zeldin, 2004, p. 80). For young people to be part of the post-conflict reconstruction period, it is required that they participate in community entrepreneurship and livelihood initiatives through capacity building, training, and regular workshops (Cafe, 2019). These types of participation do not only include youth training, but rather listening to their voice and making them part of the reconstruction projects to be decision-makers in their societies (Almasri, 2020).

Undermining sustainable development

It is very important to note here that youths were absent from the reconstruction initiatives in the Gaza Strip – not only youth but all segments of society, because it was clear that those who controlled the reconstruction process such as the PA, international organizations, Israel, and the Hamas government, were not adhering to the UN's Sustainable Development Goals in the Gaza Strip (Rukba, 2020). The focus of donor countries and organizations providing humanitarian aid to the Palestinians was on providing immediate relief, instead of long-term recovery, whether it was deliberate or not, and the conditional aid policy imposed on the Palestinians after the signing of the Oslo Accord in 1993, has created a dependent economic structure which relies on humanitarian assistance and foreign aid, leading to a dampening of any possibility of sustainable development in Palestine. The youth's exclusion from the reconstruction process is a denial of their participation in sustainable development goals; these are goals that can only be achieved through the community participation and at the highest levels (Rukba, 2020).

Also, several items of research show that "participation can strengthen social development, build organizational capacity, and create changes in the environment" (Checkoway and Gutierrez, 2008, p. 2). When there is a chance for the young to engage with peers and friends in an organized and secure environment, receive emotional support from elders, and experience a sense of community, they are more likely to remain involved and achieve satisfactory outcomes (Zeldin, 2004, p. 76). Young people have unique insights about their own challenges and resources; they also have energy and creativity (Campbell and Erbstein, 2012, p. 74).

Conclusion

Although Gaza's reconstruction was implemented through numerous actors such as UNRWA, UNDP, PA, NGOs, and construction companies (Barakat et al., 2018), the reconstruction initiatives were lacking good long-term planning, which many academics argue that this kind of planning excludes the young component from the entire process. At the decision-making stage, Palestinian youth did not participate in the development of the reconstruction strategy, they were only engaged as workers in the material reconstruction within the scope of the construction firms who have associated with the government or donors with contracts to implement the reconstruction of houses, schools, mosques, etc.

Young people must be included within a national strategic plan that provides projects and initiatives related to young people to guarantee sustainable employment opportunities through the encouragement of innovation to create creative ideas that make youths an active part in the process of development in their communities. The Gaza Strip is still suffering from Israeli occupation and the imposed siege, but there is a space where young people can play an important role to develop their lives and community through the reconstruction process. Youth participation in reconstruction initiatives is primarily an empowering process because it gives young people the necessary experience in leading peace operations and community development. Meanwhile, polls revealed that one out of three young people have the intention to leave the Gaza strip because of the dire situation that Gaza suffers in all aspects of life (PCBS, 2017). With no active youth participation in the reconstruction efforts, it seems that they will continue to lose opportunities to improve their livelihood and their society.

The consideration of young people as a vital part of the reconstruction operations gives them the chance to create opportunities that allow them to participate in achieving sustainable development in their communities. We need to find out about "young people's roles as social connectors and ideological reproducers who make, shape, and pass on social meaning" (McEvoy-Levy, 2014, para. 24). This is beneficial to build a culture of youth inclusion in political negotiations, peace processes, and in transitional justice and reconstruction efforts (McEvoy-Levy, 2014, para. 25).

References

Arab, T. N. (2019). *Palestinians are Leaving Gaza, Fleeing a Repressive Hamas Administration and Endless Wars*. Retrieved from https://english.alaraby.co.uk /english/indepth/2019/12/3/facing-years-of-repression-palestinians-continue-to -flee-gaza.

Barakat, S. (2005a). *After the Conflict: Reconstruction and Development in the Aftermath of War*. London: I. B. Tauris & Co Ltd.

Barakat, S. (2005b). Post-Saddam Iraq: deconstructing a regime, reconstructing a nation. *Third World Quarterly, 26*(4–5), 571–591.

Barakat, S. and Zyck, S. A. (2009). The Evolution of Post-conflict. *Third World Quarterly, 30*(6), 1069–1086.

Barakat, S., Milton, S., and Ghassan Elkahlout. (2018). The Gaza Reconstruction Mechanism: Old Wine in New Bottlenecks. *Journal of Intervention and Statebuilding*, 208–227.

Cafe, T. Y. (2019). *Deconstructing the Rule of Youth in Peace Building: youth Peacebuilding in Practice*. Retrieved from The Youth Cafe: https://bit.ly /2zGpmip.

Campbell, D. and Nancy Erbstein. (2012). Engaging youth in community change: three key implementation principles. *Community Development, 43*(1), 63–79.

Chandy, L. (2011). It's complicated: The challenge of implementing the Paris declaration on aid effectiveness. *Global Economy and Development at Brookings Blog 22*. Retrieved from https://pdfs.semanticscholar.org/269d/831845d1418 2d64a8018439e53ae7c99b99d.pdf.

Checkoway, B. N. and Lorraine M. Gutierrez. (2008). Youth participation and community change. *Journal of Community Practice, 14*(1–2), 1–9. DOI: 10.1300/ J125v14n01_01.

Chomsky, N. and Pappé, I. (2013). *Gaza in crisis: reflections on Israel's war against the Palestinians*. Haymarket books.

Clarke, M., Fanany, I., and Kenny, S. (Eds) (2010). *Post-Disaster Reconstruction: Lessons from Aceh*. Earthscan. Retrieved from https://bit.ly/3hOQ1eb.

Da'na, T. (2014). Disconnecting civil society from its historical extension: NGOs and neoliberalism in palestine. *Human Rights, Human Security, and State Security: The Intersection*, pp. 117–138.

Date-Bah, E. (2003). *Jobs After War: A Critical Challenge in the Peace and Reconstruction Puzzle*. International Labour Organization.

Erakat, N. (2019). *Justice for Some: Law and the Question of Palestine*. Stanford University Press.

Gennip, J. V. (2005). *Post-conflict Reconstruction and Development*. Society for International Developmen, pp. 57–62. Retrieved from https://link.springer.com/content/pdf/10.1057/palgrave.development.1100158.pdf.

Gisha (2011, November). *Scale od Control: Israel's Continued Responsibility in the Gaza Strip*. Gisha: Legal Center for Freedom of Movement.

Høigilt, J., Atallah, A., and el-Dada, H. (2013, June). Palestinian youth activism: new actors, new possibilities? *The Norwegian Peacebuilding Resource Centre (NOREF)*. Retrieved from https://www.files.ethz.ch/isn/165694/b0c26f88591 1e090b61db9089ed8040a.pdf.

Holmes, O. (2019). *Hamas violently suppresses Gaza economic protests*. The Guardian. Retrieved August 13, 2020, from https://www.theguardian.com/world/2019/mar/21/hamas-violently-suppresses-gaza-economic-israeli-border-protests.

Institute of Community and Public Health: Birzeit University (2018). The Realities of Youth in the occupied Palestinian territory. Retrieved from http://icph.birzeit.edu/news/realities-youth-occupied-palestinian-territory.

Interpeace and United Nations (2017). *Palestinian Youth Challenges and Aspirations: A Study on Youth, Peace and Security Based on UN Resolution 2250*. Palestine: Interpeace and United Nations. Retrieved from https://www.interpeace.org/wp-content/uploads/2018/04/2018-IP-case-study-Palestine-v3.pdf.

MAS (2019). *Brain Drain from the Gaza Strip: Repercussions and Possible Solutions*. Background Paper. Retrieved from http://www.mas.ps/files/server/20190812102935-1.pdf.

McEvoy-Levy, S. (2014a). Retrieved from UNICEF: Office of research-Innocenti: https://bit.ly/3fGXJ8n.

McEvoy-Levy, S. (2014b). *Youth and the Challenges of 'Post-Conflict' Peacebuilding*. UNICEF Office of Research – Innocenti. Retrieved from https://www.unicef-irc.org/article/1067-youth-and-the-challenges-of-post-conflict-peacebuilding.html.

Middle East Monitor (MEMO). (2019, December 27). *Gaza Halts Great March of Return for Three Months*. Retrieved January 6, 2021, from Middle Easet Monitor (MEMO): https://bit.ly/396pxRB.

Middle East Monitor (2018). *Lieberman tells Gaza: Overthrow Hamas to become 'Singapore of Middle East.'* Retrieved from MEMO: https://www.middleeastmonitor.com/20180725-lieberman-tells-gaza-overthrow-hamas-to-become-singapore-of-middle-east/.

O'Brien, S. (2014). *Questioning the Marshall Plan in the Buildup to the Cold War.* Retrieved from The University of New Hampshire: Inquiry Journal: https://www .unh.edu/inquiryjournal/spring-2014/questioning-marshall-plan-buildup-cold -war.

OCHA (2020). *Two Years On: People Injured and Traumatized during the "Great March of Return" Are Still Struggling.* United Nations Office for the Coordination of Humanitarian Affairs (OCHA). Retrieved from https://www.ochaopt.org/ content/two-years-people-injured-and-traumatized-during-great-march-return -are-still-struggling.

Palestinian Central Bureau of Statistics (PCBS) (2017). *PCBS: On The Eve Of International Youth Day*, August 12, 2017. Retrieved from Palestinian Central Bureau of Statistics (PCBS): http://www.pcbs.gov.ps/post.aspx?lang=en &ItemID=2048#.

PCHR (2020). *Human Rights Organisations Send Joint Written Submission on Israeli Apartheid to the UN Human Rights Council.* Gaza Strip: Palestinian Centre for Human Rights (PCHR). Retrieved from https://www.pchrgaza.org/ en/?p=14147.

Rahman, O. (2019, December 12). From confusion to clarity: three pillars for revitalizing the Palestinian national movement. *Brookings (blog).* Retrieved from https://www.brookings.edu/research/from-confusion-to-clarity/.

Schwartz, S. (2010). *Youth and Post-Conflict Reconstruction: Agents* of Change. US Institute of Peace Press.

Swart, M. (2019). *Palestinian Reconciliation and the Potential of Transitional Justice.* Doha: Brookings Doha Center. Retrieved from https://www.brookings .edu/wp-content/uploads/2019/03/Palestinian_Reconciliation_Transitional _Justice_English.pdf.

UNDP (2006). *Youth and Violent Conflict: Society and Development in Crisis?* New York: United Nations Development Programme (UNDP). Retrieved from https:// reliefweb.int/sites/reliefweb.int/files/resources/810B078967D17D1AC125719 20052088C-UNDP%20youth.pdf.

UNITAR (2014). *Impact of the 2014 Conflict in the Gaza Strip.* United Nations Institute for Training and Research (UNITAR). Retrieved June 28, 2020, from https://unosat.web.cern.ch/unosat/unitar/publications/UNOSAT_GAZA _REPORT_OCT2014_WEB.pdf.

UNRWA (2019). *Gaza's "Great March of Return" One Year On.* UNRWA.

Wilson, T. (1977). *The Marshall Plan 1947–1951.* Foreign Policy Association. Retrieved from https://bit.ly/3mvutEx.

World Bank (2019). *Palestine's Economic Update.* Retrieved June 26, 2020, from https://bit.ly/2UNMiEz.

Zeldin, S. (2004). Youth as agents of adult and community development: mapping the processes and outcomes of youth engaged in organizational governance. *Applied Developmental Science*, *8*(2), 72–90, DOI: 10.1207/s1532480xads0802_2.

Zureik, E. (2018). Qatar's humanitarian aid to Palestine. *Third World Quarterly*, *39*(4), 786–798, DOI: 10.1080/01436597.2017.1392087.

Zyck, S. A. (2016). *Never Too Early to Plan: Lessons Learned for the Post-Agreement Reconstruction of Syria.* UNDP RBAS Sub-regional Response Facility for the Syria Crisis.

Conclusion

Young people's future direction and engagement

Ibrahim Natil

This book presents a new approach to civil society in the global context by focussing on youth civic engagement and local peacebuilding. This approach is particularly strong because it is based not only on empirical discussions of individual countries but also on a firm theoretical framework of the discussion of youth civic engagement and development issues. In this way, the book significantly contributes to theoretical discussions of the complexities of political, social, and financial shifts at the global level. It also brings together scholars from the MENA region and features a range of contributions from authors at different stages of their careers, including early career scholars. A plurality of voices in this space is a strength. Most of the contributions included in the book are written by young scholars from various locations who look at the challenges facing youth in the development process. The different chapters introduce the challenges facing youth civic engagement and local peacebuilding owing to social, political, security, and health issues, such as COVID-19 in Iran. However, the book distinguishes itself as a new contribution to the field of knowledge about youth civic engagement and peacebuilding in MENA and provides some up-to-date research from young scholars from Morocco, Yemen, Syria, Iran, and Palestine, who have reflected on their experiences of researching and engaging with young people to document their impact on community development perspectives and initiatives and local peacebuilding.

Their debates and arguments are supported by fieldwork, participatory observation, interviews, and references to existing literature. This book thus situates itself in the existing literature and engages meaningfully with current debates and discussions in the established literature. The quality of its research assists the reader to understand the contributions of young people from MENA and their civil society organizations' (CSOs) interventions and endeavours to encourage young people's grassroots engagement, activism, and resilience. In other words, the reader can thereby understand the local political, social, and financial contexts, owing to the cultural and social backgrounds of youth CSOs and their social and civic opportunities and community development prospects and challenges. It also makes a contribution to the field through the inclusion of timely empirical case studies that are the foci of various chapters, including the conflicts in Syria and Yemen and the impacts of the Covid-19 pandemic, as well as paying attention to long-running conflicts and forms of insecurity. It delivers the premise that the youth and their contributions must be taken seriously by CSOs and local peacebuilding efforts. Often overlooked, the youth are actively engaging in peacebuilding and negotiating in incredibly complex and risky everyday contexts. There is a persistent belief that young people are not worth engaging or studying, but this view is increasingly changing, and books such as this will contribute to demonstrating and counteracting such opinions with evidence-based scholarship.

In brief, this book brings a heightened awareness of the challenges facing the youth as well as highlighting the potential for greater policy engagement for them to make great contributions to changing policies, e.g., eradicating poverty. The main contribution of the book is in its undertaking of new research, particularly around informed practice on the ground and presenting recommendations to policymakers and donors on better ways of providing enough space for young people and their CSOs to make contributions on specific policy issues through local and national platforms and networks.

Platforms and networks

A number of scholars, activists, community assessors, researchers, and evaluators have attempted to assess whether youth CSOs' actions are relevant to the promotion of young people's engagement in local networks. They also assessed whether CSOs' actions stimulate a local and/or national debate between young people and policymakers, focussing on the themes of active engagement in decision-making processes at all levels in MENA countries such as Palestine, Yemen, Morocco, etc. This is to ensure that local/national youth organizations achieve their goals of keeping young leaders' and activists' civic engagement, active community participation, and leadership as their main target group actions. For example, the peaceful rallies led by Yemeni women and young people to confront the authoritarian regime marked the beginning of a social transformation in relation to increased female activism in the country. The subsequent surge in female participation during the transition process supports the notion of Yemen's political and social transformation. At the National Dialogue Conference (NDC), which provided a platform to discuss visions for a new Yemen, scenes of women arguing with well-known sheikhs indicated a breakaway from the era of marginalization that subdued Yemeni women. Unfortunately, the transition process failed, and war broke out between the parties that were involved at the NDC.

Some CSOs also employ the media to promote people's rights to participate and contribute to the development of their societies by producing and broadcasting weekly, bi-monthly, and monthly live or recorded TV and radio programmes. CSOs, however, are an essential force for generating unique positive impressions. Young people, for example, use new communication technologies and social media platforms to raise the issue of their rights instead of established information networks. Social media networks are used for the promotion and distribution of the concepts of active participation in decision-making processes. However, no single institution or agency dominates social or political life or should work as the only legitimate arbiter of norms. The linkage between activism and democratization is symmetrical and reciprocal. Democracy paves the ground for activism, and in turn, activism enhances democracy's promotion. In other words, activism flourishes in democratic political systems, and democracy is promoted and enhanced through committed activism. It should also be said that any type of activism presupposes the existence of civic engagement as a precondition for its survival, as discussed by the contributors from Morocco in Chapter 4.

In other words, young people should be engaged in designing, broadcasting, and circulating materials as well as organizing activities to foster a free press in their efforts to eliminate the technical and cultural obstacles that they face in their contributions to public life. This is to allow the discussion of certain concepts of civic engagement and community participation in policy- and decision-making processes as a central theme to raise public awareness with respect to vulnerable and marginalized groups' rights. However, political activism flourishes only when individuals are active and willing to contribute for the benefit and progress of their society, when they voluntarily relate to each other on the basis of shared interests. Also, civility implies tolerance – that is, respect for different points of view and social attitudes – and requires regularity of behaviour, rules of conduct, and respect for the law as well as for the individual's autonomy, which is based on trust among people who perhaps never meet, as discussed in Chapter 5.

One example is youth CSOs' use of a new approach of assisting activists to form community forums or platforms to increase the scope of their engagement with and intervention in their community issues and problems. For example, CSOs have implemented grassroots initiatives and projects to train young leaders to practise their new skills through local engagement and contributions in the post-conflict Gaza Strip since 2014, as discussed in Chapters 2 and 9. Young people's leaders selected their representatives to lead grassroots initiatives for social and political representation at the local level despite the different constraints and challenges they faced. They may assess and monitor the performances of social services, despite being practically discriminated against by politicians with very narrow political interests and are seeking to achieve success regardless through good governance practices, active grassroots engagement and community participation, and effective leadership.

Leadership challenges

Despite the challenges of culture, political structures, and crises of leadership in local activism and grassroots groups, there are women who are still fighting for effective engagement in political, social, and civil rights and responsibilities. Young activists are equally undertaking social and traditional responsibilities and duties at the grassroots level. However, society generally prefers a man in both the public and private spheres. Some groups do not have the capacity to maintain themselves and challenge the social, economic, financial, and political pressures or even have mechanisms to become involved in the policymaking processes of poverty alleviation and civil society empowerment. Young people, including young women, still face a great deal of social, economic, and political challenges that hinder them from obtaining their full rights. A number of active youth CSOs are enhancing civic engagement and active participation through grassroots networks supporting their endeavours. This includes broadcasting and circulating materials and organizing activities to foster a free press and civic engagement in the public policy agenda.

Youth CSOs' and grassroots groups' deliveries and interventions to promote young people's engagement in community peacebuilding and/or peacemaking will contribute to increasing their participation in the social, economic, cultural, and political development processes of society. Young leaders also should be actively engaged to influence the media, whether print or audio, television or electronic. This would guarantee the peace and security of local citizens and remove all forms of incitement, hatred, and conflict. However, the "peace process" in Yemen does not fully include all segments of Yemeni society and the youth in particular, as Elham Raweh discussed in Chapter 8. Young people are the future of the country, so this process will surely be fragile, and violence will be likely to break out again in the future if young people are not fully integrated. This requires international organizations such as the UN and CSOs to work together to promote the concepts and practices of young people's engagement in community peace and dialogue. This may lead to the discovery of new prospects for dialogue among activists based on public interests, not on narrow ones. Young people also spread a culture of community peace among all members of the local community, especially women. They engage in activities of respecting political pluralism in society, something that would raise the level of democracy and help social, cultural, and political groups and institutions succeed. This will increase their level of leadership by organizing meetings and dialogue to tackle the challenges facing community peacebuilding and reconciliation at the internal level.

Young people's engagement will assist with being to open to others and reinforcing a culture of bilateral relations, respect for others' opinions, exchange of thoughts and expertise for the sake of society. This will assist young people in reinforcing a culture of dialogue among members of the local community, given the fact that dialogue is important for the sake of connectivity and mutual respect within the framework of the national interests. Dialogue should be promoted, especially among citizens. Local organizations should cooperate and coordinate more with each other for the benefit of community peacebuilding. Media outlets should start adopting some strategies that would enhance reconciliation and end political division in cooperation with the local government and education departments to introduce special programmes or activities in schools, promoting the principles of reconciliation, dialogue, and community peacebuilding. There have been a number of CSOs trying to contribute to the promotion of grassroots engagement in decision-making processes and to increase their power. Women's groups who actively participated in popular and collective public activities to get rid of the regime in Yemen are a good example of such engagement and of people deciding on their own future. However, the direct participation of some women's groups, such as the Houthi women calling themselves "*Al-Zainabiyat*," in violent conflict is a breakaway from established and imposed local social norms, as Belal Abdo, Abdulrahman Abohajeb, and Ala Mohsen discussed in Chapter 7.

Young women's engagement in peaceful activities run by local CSOs may contribute to promoting values and practices of dialogue and women's grassroots participation in community peacebuilding actions. Young leaders may attempt to become engaged in activities if they had opportunities to participate in well-designed civil society activities for the purpose of changing their behaviours and attitudes to promote and respect peacebuilding, conflict resolution, and peace processes. Young leaders should understand the impact of non-violence, dialogue, and peaceful actions in society as these are essential components of the participatory approach to contributing to their society's community peacebuilding despite the existence of violence, division, and high levels of poverty. Some CSO teams, for example, should run regular follow-up activities such as workshops, public awareness sessions, town hall meetings, seminars, conferences, interviews, and field visits at a variety of locations to ensure the effectiveness of their young people's engagement. These activities would make it possible for staff to remain very close to the needs, views, and issues of young people. CSOs' staff should encourage beneficiaries and young people's groups under different civic engagement and community participation themes to assess their needs and the issues to be tackled and addressed in the planning of future activities. They should also seek to strengthen mutual relationships with these different young groups, who often express their needs and views freely. This close relationship with young people would provide staff with a remarkable knowledge and understanding of the different needs and issues of target groups.

Peacebuilding challenges

In addition to women's engagement in violence and the exclusion of young people from the "peace process" in Yemen, the question of child soldiers (15–17 years old) remains a real challenge for future local peacebuilding in many countries such as Iraq and Libya, as Yousra Hasona discussed in Chapter 6. This has become a serious issue due to its imposing a threat to the "peace process" and stability in the post-war phase. Governments should develop a plan and approaches to engage this age group with their societies and to integrate them without stigmatization or rejection. MENA countries should encourage engaging young people in civil society to ensure that development priorities are based on a broad consensus in society. Marginalized and vulnerable young people still need to get engaged in a fully participatory process as an integral part of the agenda for development, peace, and democracy. A key methodology is to engage participants by planning, designing, and implementing a national plan that relies mainly on a participatory approach and process from bottom to top. This should start with local grassroots organizations advocating for the public on their needs in the policy-making process. Local women leaders, young graduates, and other women and CSOs should be able to become involved in the implementation of the national plan.

In order to strengthen youth civic engagement, youth CSOs should consider the use of a very closely engaged process with the community to assess the needs of young people and beneficiaries who participated actively in the planning of programmes. For example, local youth groups should keep working closely and on a regular basis with different young people's target groups in designing and implementing different projects. However, conflict remains a major barrier to empowering and improving the skills of young people and their civic engagement and local peacebuilding initiatives. The Syrian conflict, for example, has left thousands of people, killed, displaced, and detained. Young people formed various groups of volunteers to help their societies; however, their voluntary actions were not welcomed owing to the political environment, as Alaa Hadid discussed in Chapter 5.

These challenges give opportunities for scholars and practitioners to understand and explore the potential impact of these issues on young people's civic engagement in the short and long run by conducting future research.

Ways forward

This is a growing area of attention, in which more scholarship is needed. Future research should consider the methods that are used by local youth groups. Researchers should identify the tools of the youth for planning, monitoring, evaluation, and research purposes to explore certain information and assess the impact of their activities on target groups. The research and evaluation tools are used to study certain problems and explore their solutions. Some CSOs, however, also use field monitoring to envision changes for active civic engagement and participation, premised on long-term involvement. Some youth CSOs, for example, monitor the services delivered by local organizations and seek to monitor the services of local councils. Researchers should identify that certain activities are monitored by young people to ensure human rights standards are respected by state and non-state actors. Field surveys are used to share information with the public and enrich those civil society materials focussing on the values of active community participation and civic engagement. Their results help to clarify whether the objectives of the activities have been fully met. Written evaluations also provide feedback on the activity's next steps and how participants envision the implementation of skills, the running of the peacebuilding and development actions, and campaigning activities.

Young people and their CSOs should engage with different sectors and discuss these with experts to learn and practise various concepts of communication, dialogue, tolerance, and community reconciliation in areas where conflict divides societies, such as Yemen, Palestine, Libya, Syria, and Iraq. CSOs should take advance action to engage young people to promote a culture of community peace and peacebuilding through a number of creative cultural activities. Cooperation among CSOs, however, is essential to enhancing self-confidence and an active grassroots level in social and political actions that would promote the role of different sectors of society in curbing violence and empowering human rights practices. The role of young people's CSOs should promote a culture of conflict resolution and peacebuilding, as well as the impact of the social context on peacebuilding. They must promote and raise young people's awareness, empower their abilities, and invest in their energies. They must effectively contribute to achieving and building the best future for concepts of civil peace and to consolidating many of the concepts and positive values that contribute to the construction of a civil society. These activities would contribute to challenging violence and its impact on the practices of young people's engagement in human rights development and good governance practices.

Future research may consider exploring young people's leadership in CSOs to explore political, social, and economic dynamics and structures that influence the leadership of CSOs at the local, national, and global levels. It should focus on challenges facing CSOs' societal contributions, current operational practices, and strategies for future development. This will assist with the general understanding of CSOs, which play an increasingly important role in the political, economic, and social dynamics that shape daily lives across the world.

This research area may provide overviews of some international actors' interests and values in supporting civil society projects. Scholars may examine the impact of CSOs on local politics, power, and social and political life. They may also explore the lessons learnt from certain leaders or civil society groups despite divisions, violence, social conservatism, lack of opportunities, and the role of various political systems in this regard. These experiences and case studies of leaders' performances, challenges, and engagement in the activities of CSOs can be examined. These may include the following areas:

- Leadership and civic engagement challenges
- Language challenges and educational initiatives
- Young people's leadership in civil society
- Challenges and changes caused by COVID-19
- Challenges caused by foreign aid and financial shifts
- Community development leadership
- Leadership in local peacebuilding
- Leadership and social media challenges in conflict zones
- Community peacebuilding and leadership in non-violence initiatives
- Leadership in human rights and advocacy campaigns
- Challenges facing social movements/civil society leadership

Research in these areas will assist young scholars and practitioners from different parts of the world to promote cooperation between societies and communities across the world so as to advance our understanding of how CSOs' young leaders can contribute to making societies more just and equal.

Index

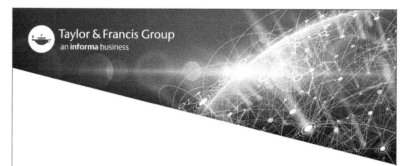